TIME TO SELL?

GUIDE TO SELLING A PHYSICIAN PRACTICE:
VALUE, OPTIONS, ALTERNATIVES

By Randy Bauman

Published by Greenbranch Publishing, LLC
PO Box 208
Phoenix, MD 21131
Phone: (800) 933-3711
Fax: (410) 329-1510
Email: info@greenbranch.com
Website: www.mpmnetwork.com, www.soundpractice.net

This publication is designed to provide general medical practice management information and is sold with the understanding that neither the author nor the publisher is engaged in rendering legal, accounting, ethical, or clinical advice. If legal or other expert advice is required, the services of a competent professional person should be sought.

CPT® is a registered trademark of the American Medical Association

Printed in the United States of America by United Book Press, Inc. www.unitedbookpress.com

PUBLISHER
Nancy Collins

EDITORIAL ASSISTANT
Jennifer Weiss

BOOK DESIGNER
Laura Carter
Carter Publishing Studio

COVER DESIGN
Jim Dodson
Carter Publishing Studio

INDEX
Paul Hightower

COPYEDITOR
Hearthside Publishing Services

Table of Contents

Dedication

To my daughter Arial.
May the bright sun and the gift of knowledge always shine on you.

Acknowledgements

Writing is a cathartic experience. It requires taking the time to put in words experiences, observations, and perspectives in a way we rarely are required to do. It forces organization of thoughts, analysis of trends, and consideration of options and alternatives. It requires expressing an opinion. The process made me a better trusted advisor to my clients.

Thanks to Carla Hall for all of her encouragement, suggestions, and world-class proofreading skills (and for driving the truck).

Thanks to Angela Herron and Leif Beck for reading the manuscript and providing excellent comments and suggestions that made this a better book.

Thanks to Daryl Demonbreun, my business partner, for always being there.

Thanks to Bob Maier, who took a chance on a green kid and taught him about health care.

Finally, thank you to Nancy Collins at Greenbranch Publishing for her encouragement, support, and suggestions and to all the folks at Greenbranch who helped make this book a reality.

Randy Bauman
October, 2008

About the Author

Randy Bauman is president of Delta Health Care (www.deltahealthcare.com) in Brentwood, Tennessee. For more than 20 years, Randy has advised physician groups and hospitals on the business of physician practice, including group practice development, strategic planning, mergers and acquisitions, group formations, compensation, governance, operations, and practice valuations.

At Delta Health Care, he developed models and processes the company uses to merge small physician practices into mega-groups. The firm has established a national reputation as group practice merger experts, having completed multiple mergers of more than 50 physicians. Those groups are now some of the largest and most successful physician groups in the country.

His articles and speeches at times challenge conventional wisdom on emerging healthcare trends and practices. When he wrote "Diddling the Overhead" to cajole physicians out of their often-singular focus on cost, the article was rejected by several national publications as "too controversial." He published it in Delta's company newsletter. It subsequently was picked up by others in the industry and found a national Internet audience.

He is a frequent speaker at Medical Group Management Association (MGMA) and Healthcare Financial Management Association (HFMA) chapters and has presented numerous audio conferences on a diverse range of topics such as *The Changing Hospital/Physician Relationship*, *Reality Check—I'm Not in Control of My Practice*, and *Disruptive Physicians and How to Deal with Them*.

He has been interviewed by and had articles published in numerous healthcare publications including *The Journal of Medical Practice Management*, *Medical Economics*, *The Physician's Advisory*, *Doctor's Digest*, *Unique Opportunities*, *ACP Observer*, *The Journal of Family Practice*, and *Group Practice Solutions*.

He lives in Sandia Park, New Mexico, and in his spare time he pursues his passions for landscape photography and motorcycling. His award-winning photographs are available at galleries and other venues in the greater Albuquerque area.

Foreword

Americans receive the best health care in the world. Our physicians are superbly trained, committed to giving conscientious, highly specialized care while being personally concerned for patients' welfare. Our hospitals are technical marvels spawned by a huge supply of both financial and human capital.

Still, at least at the doctor level, we just can't seem to get it right. Various social and political forces threaten to kill the will of this most essential healthcare component—the physicians who provide the brains and judgment to diagnose and treat an incredible variety of patient problems.

Having consulted to so many of these fine people for some 37 years, I stand in both awe of and distress for them. How, I wonder, can so many highly able providers of top-quality care do so much good on an individual basis and yet struggle so much to make their personal and financial lives acceptable? And how can it be that, while physicians in some specialties are highly successful economically, a growing number of others just aren't making it?

Randy Bauman, author of this fine book, can't, of course, answer those overriding questions any better than anyone else. But having known and worked with so many medical practice advisors over the years, I've come to respect his technical abilities and his practical judgment in working with medical practices and their physician-members. He has seen and dealt with it all, honestly and openly, with (mostly) excellent results for his clients.

One of the issues he's dealt with extensively the past few years is the subject of this book. The idea of selling out was oddly popular back in the mid and late 1990s because both hospitals and physician practice management companies (PPMCs) were offering what quickly turned out to be foolishly high prices. Randy and I, and indeed almost all medical consultants, went through that period when some doctors sold out "at the top." Not more than a couple of years later, the hospitals and PPMCs discovered their overgenerosity and resold many of those practices back at huge losses.

This time around, things are different. Some physicians and groups can command surprisingly high prices. For many others doctors, the economics may or may not be there. Doctors see ever increasing regulation, decreasing reimbursement, and heavy fixed costs (including malpractice insurance) bearing down on them both financially and emotionally. The situation leads more of them than ever to say, "I just want to get out of the business and simply take care of patients." Selling out is an increasingly popular option, but whether it's for you and, if so, how to go about it is not a simple matter.

Randy has been heavily involved in advising whether doctors should (or can) sell their practices and, if yes, how to do it and at what price. Reading this book, I can just see and hear Randy giving the "real skinny" in reply to questions about selling out. No book I know of has more direct talk, honest, down-to-earth advice on the subject.

Time to Sell? Guide to Selling a Physician Practice: Value, Options, Alternatives deals with all the aspects of the urge to sell. It starts right in with the first—and major—question: Why do you want to sell, and is such an action the right thing for you? He ends the book by coming back to that basic question, forthrightly discussing your other options for much the same reason—that selling out must fit the doctor personally even more so than on the technical issues. I've worked with Randy enough times to know how much the personally "right" result matters to him.

In between these two bookends, Chapters 2 though 7 offer sophisticated advice in a down-to-earth, understandable way. I've struggled sometimes to explain ideas like the discounted cash flow approach in helping set an asking price, but—having been through it literally hundreds of times—Randy makes it understandable. Then in Chapters 5, 6 and 7, he takes it past the valuation question by coaching how to make the deal. After all, having a price and negotiating a result are two vastly different matters, each calling for special attention.

And to help ensure that the reader gets it, *Time to Sell? Guide to Selling a Physician Practice: Value, Options, Alternatives* lists specific Takeaway Points and checklists at the end of each chapter.

Randy is not an attorney and, although I am, it's good that he isn't. While you absolutely need a well-qualified lawyer to finalize the sale, I've seen lawyers kill too many desirable medical practice deals. *Time to Sell? Guide to Selling a Physician Practice: Value, Options, Alternatives* recognizes the legal formalities but, more importantly, serves as a practical guide to help you reach the best possible results *for you*.

You, after all, have to make the right judgments, not your lawyer, consultant, or other advisors. By reading this book carefully you should feel well-prepared to deal with an issue that is rising more quickly than you may realize.

Leif C. Beck, JD, CHBC
Founder and Former Publisher of "Physicians' Advisory"
and "Group Practice Success" Newsletters,
and Medical Management Consultant

Introduction

Trends, like horses, are easier to ride in the direction they are going.

JOHN NAISBITT

The trend is unmistakable—physicians are selling their practices at a feverish pace. In my role as a practice consultant, working with both hospitals and physician practices, I can tell you this trend is taking on tsunami proportions. It is refreshing and disturbing at the same time. Many physicians struggle with running their own businesses and are giving up. This guide should prove an invaluable resource for identifying what is wrong with their practice and pointing them in the right direction for future success whether they decide to sell or not.

In some parts of the country, a vast majority of formerly independent physician practices are now owned—and the physicians employed—by large hospital systems. In others, the physicians are the pursuers—lining up at the hospital administrator's door offering to sell their practice. The activity is just beginning in some communities, but rare is a community where the trend isn't present.

The quote from management guru John Naisbitt, above, illustrates that trends tend to take on a life of their own. There is a bit of lemming behavior in most business trends, and those of us in the healthcare industry saw a similar trend of hospitals buying physician practices unfold and reach fever proportions in the 1990s. The existence of a clear trend does not assure the success of the underlying strategy, so caution is in order.

This guide's purpose is to walk physicians and practice managers through the process of objectively evaluating a practice and determining whether selling is the right option. Each chapter covers a step in the process and contains practical advice, pitfalls, questions, and checklists.

CHAPTER 1

Why Sell?

I always have to remind myself that it's never as good as it seems on the best days and never as bad as it seems on the worst days. That's how I keep my perspective.   ANONYMOUS PHYSICIAN

A medical practice is a small business and running a small business, especially in medicine, has become increasingly complex. Regulatory compliance, declining and uncertain reimbursement, restrictions on ancillary services, physician shortages and rapidly increasing starting salaries, and rising malpractice premiums are just some of the things that seem to be conspiring to make private practices difficult to sustain. No wonder the unmistakable trend is practices selling to hospitals.

Let's look at some of these issues in more detail:

REGULATION

Federal, state, and local laws seem designed to make running a small business difficult. Beyond normal regulatory compliance such as tax, pension, wage and hour laws, etc., healthcare has its own set of additional regulations that add complexity. For example, consider some of the laws and complex regulations that apply to even the smallest medical practices:

- OSHA—the Occupational Safety and Health Administration
- CLIA—Clinical Laboratory Improvement Amendments
- HIPAA—Health Insurance Portability and Accountability Act
- Medicare (billing, coding, unbundling, supervision requirements, etc.)
- State Medicaid regulations and eligibility requirements
- Third-party payor rules and regulations, which often vary from Medicare
- Self referral (the Stark Law)

There is no exemption from complying with these and other regulations and the penalties are often quite harsh.

REIMBURSEMENT

Starting back in the mid-1980s, commercial insurance companies began developing networks of physicians. They promised reduced paperwork and streamlined payments. No longer would the physician bill the patient who would, in turn, file a claim with the insurance company. Instead, the patient would pay a nominal co-payment, and the physician would bill the insurance company and be paid based on a predetermined fee schedule.

The result was that it became easier for insurance companies to market their networks of physicians to employers and sell their insurance products. It sounded like a good deal to the physicians, too—just bill the insurance companies rather than hundreds of individual patients.

Over the years, smaller insurance companies were purchased by larger insurance companies. Recent years have seen mergers of these large insurance companies to the point that many areas of the country are now dominated by a small number of commercial third-party payors. These payors basically control a medical group's commercial patients and wield tremendous market power.

While payments to physician practices were to be based on a negotiated fee schedule, in reality there is very little negotiation. Many physician groups have two options: accept the fee schedule being offered or lose the business.

A couple of years ago, I worked with a business-astute solo family physician in the northeast. He knew something was wrong in his practice—he was working harder and making less. He went back and traced actual payments from one of his main commercial payors over the preceding six-year period. He found an average decline of 4.2% per year in payment rates for his major CPT codes and an overall decline during the six-year period of more than 19%!

When he confronted the payor with this data the company shrugged and told him he was free to terminate the contract. The managed care battle has been fought, and solo and small physician groups lost. They have virtually no leverage in negotiating payment rates. They sold their patients to the insurance companies and got them back at a discount.

Medicare patients, who usually make up 30% to 60% of a physician practice, are paid for by an equally faulty system. Medicare implemented a national fee schedule in the 1990s, and physician fees are to be automatically adjusted annually based on a flawed statutory formula. The result is that Medicare operates under a perennial threat of double-digit rate cuts. As a result, in some parts of the country, physicians are limiting access or have stopped taking new Medicare patients.

A majority of commercial payors' fee schedules are based on Medicare's national fee schedule, with commercial rates set as a percentage of Medicare's. Downward pressure on Medicare fees has the prospect of reduced commercial reimbursement rates as well.

State Medicaid program rates often don't even cover the cost of providing the services and have caused large numbers of physicians to either drop Medicaid altogether or to severely limit the number of these patients they are willing to take on in their practice.

ANCILLARY SERVICES

Ancillary services such as lab and diagnostic imaging have been the staple of many successful practices. The ability to generate a profit margin from ancillary services historically can represent as much as 20% to 30% of the revenue of a primary care practice—and even more in specialty practices.

Recent years have seen reimbursement changes that make this profitable strategy less lucrative and have even lead to the shutdown of these services in some practices.

The Deficit Reduction Act of 2005, which was effective in 2007, reduced Medicare reimbursement on most diagnostic imaging procedures performed in physician offices by 25% to 30%. Commercial payors, whose reimbursement rates often are pegged to a percentage of Medicare, are following these reductions in many parts of the country.

In addition, commercial payors in some parts of the country are establishing additional requirements on in-office imaging including the following:

- A requirement that they provide a full range of imaging modalities
- A requirement for a full-time radiologist on-site
- Accreditation requirements

The cost of meeting these requirements makes it difficult, if not impossible, for smaller practices to provide these services.

RECRUITMENT AND RETENTION

Recruiting and retaining physicians is increasingly difficult. This problem is driven by three interrelated factors:

1. Physician shortages in many specialties have driven up physician starting salaries. Many physician groups are finding that the starting salary for a newly trained physician is in excess of what senior partners earn.

2. Many younger physicians have little interest in the business side of medicine and tend to be more lifestyle- and family-focused than their predecessors. They fear any uncertainty in their incomes—uncertainty tied to the performance of the practice. As a result, they shy away from becoming an owner in the practice. A stable income, regular work hours, and schedule flexibility tend to be their prime concerns and, as a result, many are attracted to hospital employment.

3. Many areas of the country have become unattractive to both younger and even well-established physicians. Third-party reimbursement rates, poor payor mix, and high malpractice insurance premiums are exacerbating physician access problems in these areas. The higher starting salaries are even harder to support, because the underlying practice economics are worse. The result is physician shortages in these areas.

All of the above factors conspire to make it seem quite compelling to sell to a hospital and become an employee. The hospital seems like a logical shelter from these uncertainties. Hospitals need physicians and have deeper pockets. They may be able to reduce some costs and realize some scale in things like malpractice insurance, and they may have more leverage in payor contracting.

SHOULD YOU SELL?

The decision to sell or not sell your practice is a complex one, and it involves much more than the financial and security considerations, which are often foremost in the mind of physicians. While these financial and security considerations are important—after all, everything has its price and everyone wants security—my experience is that, in the long run, qualitative issues are a much better predictor of satisfaction than quantitative ones.

Though the above factors provide some compelling reasons to sell, it should be noted that many physicians and physician groups, both large and small, continue not only to survive but thrive in private practice. They are likely to continue to do so in spite of the challenges above. Chapter 8 describes the traits that make these groups successful and provides options and strategies you can adopt to preserve independent private practice if you decide selling your practice is not in your best interest.

Before you go much further, take some time to step back and reflect.

- Why are you practicing medicine in your current location?
- Why are you in your current practice?
- Why are you in a solo, small group, large group, single-specialty or multi-specialty group?

- What other types of practice have you tried?

Group practice is like a marriage, and some group practices go bad just like some marriages go bad. Yet usually it isn't the institution of marriage that is the problem but rather the relationship. So why do many physicians have a bad experience in group practice and blame the group structure rather than the individuals?

There are many successful examples of single-specialty and multi-specialty groups in most parts of the country. So don't blame your experiences on the institution of group practice without reflecting on what else was at work in a bad situation. Evaluating what you like and dislike about your current structure is a critical first step.

The next questions you have to ask yourself are the following:

- What will change if your practice is sold and you become an employee of a hospital?
- Would you lose some of the things you like, such as autonomy and independence?
- Would the hospital solve some of the things you dislike?

Tread carefully. Just as having children is usually not the best way to resolve marital difficulties, selling your practice may simply move your problems into a different realm. See Checklists 1 and 2 at the end of this chapter to begin your self evaluation.

I find that many physicians lack the perspective to recognize whether the current situation is objectively good or bad. Sometimes the grass looks greener on the other side. One physician hit the nail on the head when he told me: "I always have to remind myself that it's never as good as it seems on the best days and never as bad as it seems on the worst days. That's how I keep my perspective."

Perspective on your current situation involves multiple components. I worked with an internist a few years ago who was pushing his group practice to sell to the hospital. He had a passionate list of plausible reasons why this was a good move.

After spending some time with him and each of his partners individually, I learned that the underlying issue was that this physician didn't get along with his partners or anyone else for that matter. The question wasn't whether or not they should sell. The question was how being employed by the hospital would solve their intra-group personality problems. They would still be working in the same office and sharing call—and still be financially tied together. What would change?

Many physicians think the decision to sell should be based solely on the monetary offer from the hospital because, after all, "everything has its price." This is a trap, too. As we will see in upcoming chapters, there are many things that are often more important than the monetary terms.

Selling a practice is a strategic decision, and it needs to be viewed beyond the realm of short-term financial considerations.

Takeaway Points for Chapter 1

- The trend of physicians selling is real but not without precedent.
- Independent practice faces challenges on many fronts: regulation, reimbursement, recruitment, and others.
- Evaluate your true motivation for selling and whether the sale will solve any underlying problems.
- Selling your practice is never a panacea—it never solves *all* your problems and may even introduce some new ones.

Chapter 1 Checklist 1: Potential Gains and Losses

Use this checklist to evaluate the severity of the problems you hope to solve and the relative importance of the perks you may gain or lose.

Which of these potential "reasons to sell" apply to your situation? Note specifics about how each affects your practice and with what severity.

❏ Regulation and compliance issues _____

_____

❏ Billing and management complexity _____

_____

❏ Restrictions and declining profitability of ancillary services _____

_____

❏ Lack of leverage in payor contract negotiations _____

_____

❏ Declining reimbursement and reimbursement uncertainty_____

_____

❏ Need to recruit physicians and high starting salaries/physician shortages ____

_____

How important is each potential hospital benefit to you?

❏ Professional practice management_____

_____

❏ Negotiation with third party payors _____

_____

❏ Attractive benefit packages for staff _____

_____

❑ Potentially lower malpractice rates _____

_____

❑ Retirement plans _____

_____

❑ Health insurance for you and your family _____

_____

❑ Disability insurance _____

_____

❑ Integrated electronic medical records _____

_____

❑ Sophisticated billing and collections systems _____

_____

Chapter 1 Checklist 2: Evaluating Your Readiness to Sell

Physicians become employees when a hospital owns the practice. Use the questions in this checklist to help you decide if you would be happy in that role.

❏ Are you prepared to turn over at least some control of your work schedule to fit in with the hospital's policies?

❏ Do you currently have scheduling flexibility (like leaving early on Fridays) that may not fit in with corporate expectations?

❏ Would you look forward to adopting new ways to make your practice more efficient? Or does the thought of using a new practice management system or electronic medical record system make your head ache?

❏ Do you want to learn to work in a way that pulls in more money? Or would you resent a hospital "suit" giving you guidelines for improving the number of patients you see?

❏ Are you ready and willing to trade away any upside potential for protection from downside risk?

❏ Do you hope to rid yourself of personnel decisions? Or does giving up some control of your staff feel too risky?

❏ What was your relationship with or attitude about hospital management when you were in your residency program?

❏ Do you know and respect the leadership of local hospitals?

❏ Have you talked with other physicians who have sold their practice? Do you think their good and bad experiences would apply to your situation? How?

CHAPTER 2

Preparing Your Practice for Sale

Charming home in established neighborhood. In original condition.
Needs TLC.   REAL ESTATE ADVERTISEMENT

You probably wouldn't put a "For Sale" sign in your front lawn without some preparation, and the same applies to putting your practice on the market. The biggest mistake physicians make in selling is that they jump in without adequate preparation. Planning ahead to make your business as attractive and as valuable as possible is critical. Selling a practice, like selling a house, means that taking the time to prepare it for sale can pay off handsomely.

First, step back and look at the real estate equivalent of curb appeal. How will your practice look to a potential purchaser? I have a friend who claims that all antiques become antiques only after passing through the phase where they are a "piece of junk." I see many practices with waiting rooms where the furniture and décor is in this near-antique stage.

Furniture isn't the only thing that impacts perception. Is the paint peeling off the door? Is the carpet worn and stained? Is your signage professional and visible or faded and dated? While these things may not directly impact the financial valuation of your practice, they will impact the *perception* of your practice to a potential purchaser and perception often becomes reality.

Most hospitals are very image conscious. They invest heavily in their main entrances, waiting rooms, landscaping, and even color selection in order to project a calming yet professional image. What image do they have of you and your practice?

I'm not suggesting a Taj Mahal either. I worked with one solo physician whose wife spent $50,000 decorating the waiting room. A good modern and tasteful image is what you are looking for.

When dressing up your practice for sale, don't fall into the trap of thinking you'll somehow be more attractive to a hospital if you invest in state-of-the-art technology. Technology investments have some of the shortest useful lives of any assets you will purchase. A five-year-old computer is ancient, and software depreciates at a rapid rate.

Don't invest in an expensive electronic medical records (EMR) system or new practice management software if you are planning to sell. Transitioning to a new EMR system takes valuable time and cuts into productivity, at least initially. Changing your billing system always results in short-term cash flow reductions.

The hospital you affiliate with may not use your hardware and software anyway, so your investment will have minimal value to them and you will likely have another learning curve post-acquisition.

If you do purchase other major equipment within a year or two of selling, be sure to keep good records to justify the value. Make sure these items are taken into account when your practice is being priced.

FINANCIAL PERFORMANCE

Instead of the purchases described above, concentrate on positive revenue trends and generating above-average incomes. Your financial performance is the most important aspect of your practice's value. Financial performance will drive the value of your practice, your income post-sale, and maybe even the hospital's level of interest. Many hospitals will shy away from a practice with subpar finances or practices viewed as faltering and in need of a turnaround. Financial performance can be broken down into three main components: physician income, revenue, and overhead. Let's examine each of these in more detail.

PHYSICIAN INCOME

Your income is a driving factor behind the value of your practice and is a key aspect of your preparation to sell. The compensation package you are offered by the hospital will likely be based on your current income. The hospital's ability to successfully operate your practice and manage its finances will also be driven by your income expectations.

Before you place your practice on the market—before you approach a hospital or share any financial data, you need to know how your income compares to your peers and why.

Physician income can be a bit nebulous in smaller practices. Every dollar collected that is not spent on overhead is available for physician income, but that is not necessarily what shows up on a physician's W-2 form.

Many practices have generous physician-owner benefits such as health, life, and disability insurance as well as retirement plan contributions. High levels of physician discretionary expenses such as auto expenses, meals, travel, and entertainment and continuing education also can lead to an understatement of the true earning ability of a practice.

Physician income is usually "normalized" to adjust for varying levels of these nonstandard physician benefits and other discretionary expenses so it more accurately reflects physician income. The valuation firm the hospital engages (Chapter 4) will examine and adjust for these expenses. You may need to work with your CPA or practice consultant to obtain a more accurate estimate of your earning ability. For a quick estimate, simply add any physician expenses that you feel may be a bit extravagant to your W-2 income.

Once your true earnings are estimated, compare that income to your peers. The Medical Group Management Association (MGMA—*www.mgma.com*) publishes annual surveys of physician income by specialty, group size, geographic location, and years in practice.

While the MGMA surveys are comprehensive, there are many other sources available as well. Look carefully at what they include, as many surveys reveal only income. They may not include some important information such as revenue, overhead, and staffing levels.

- Practice Support Resources, Inc. (*www.practicesupport.com*) publishes an annual *Practice Management STATS Quick Reference*.
- *Medical Economics* (*www.medicaleconomics.modernmedicine.com*) publishes annual physician salary surveys compiled from its readers.

Other noted physician salary surveys include the following:

- Sullivan, Cotter and Associates, Inc. Physician Compensation and Productivity Survey Report
- Hay Group Physicians Compensation Survey
- ECS Watson Wyatt Hospital and Health Care Management Compensation Report
- William M. Mercer Integrated Health Networks Compensation Survey

I find the MGMA surveys to be the most comprehensive, as their data sources are extensive surveys that are completed by member practices and then extensively vetted by MGMA personnel. With some of the other surveys, the data sources are sometimes not clear and the sample size may be limited. Surveys by recruiting firms are often based on recent candidate placements and may not reflect income levels of physicians in private practice.

Your state or local medical society or various specialty societies may have data as well.

Your CPA or practice consultant should have access to this information and can help you complete this comparison.

If your income, after adjustment for the discretionary expenses discussed above, is significantly below the MGMA median for your specialty in your geographic location, you need to find out why.

REVENUE

A vast majority of practices I have worked with over the past 20 years that have below-average physician incomes have revenue issues. Ideally you want to show the hospital that your revenue is average or above for your specialty and that your revenue is growing each year. This tells them that your practice is thriving, which will make your practice more attractive and support a higher valuation. Declining revenue trends, even by only 1% or 2% per year, can be construed as a declining practice.

Compare your revenue to the MGMA or other surveys. Revenue does vary, often dramatically, by geographic region so make sure your comparison is specific to your location. If your revenue is lower than that of your peers you will need to drill down to determine why. Revenue is comprised of several components which will need to be examined individually.

Productivity includes the number of patients you see, the number of procedures you perform, and the CPT® codes you apply to those patient visits and procedures. This is the component doctors can most easily impact.

The MGMA surveys publish data on the number of patient encounters. Compare the encounter data of your practice to the surveys to determine what part your personal productivity plays in your revenue.

Productivity can be below average for many reasons. You may need to look at your work schedule, time off, scheduling templates, work habits, and other factors. A degree of self-assessment may be required. Taking the time to understand your productivity now will also be helpful when it comes to negotiating with the hospital later (Chapter 6). Most hospitals will seek to base your post-sale bonus or even your base salary on your ability to maintain or attain a specified level of production.

Coding also impacts revenue. Many physicians have the propensity to under-code, often because they fear payor chart audits. Taking the time to learn and follow proper coding and documentation procedures can enhance your revenue without significant additional work—better documentation of work you are already doing can result in increases in revenue.

Some physicians are on the opposite end of this spectrum—they tend to be too aggressive in coding. This has the opposite affect as it tends to overstate revenue. Many hospitals will review your coding and documentation for compliance before the sale and monitor it for compliance post-sale. If you have a tendency to be aggressive in coding you may find your productivity declines after the sale.

Billing and collections is another revenue component. If your revenue is below average yet your productivity and coding are in line, then this is the next place to look.

The most common problems in billing and collections are in the failure to collect co-payments. Co-payments increasingly represent a huge percentage of what most physicians are paid for an office visit. They should be collected before the patient is seen. Billing patients for co-payments is inefficient and likely violates the terms of your payor contracts.

Another area you should review is your financial policies. Many practices continue to provide care to patients with significant old outstanding balances. While there are ethical concerns that need to be considered, ignoring these balances and continuing to provide care sends the wrong message. You may decide to provide some free care, but that is a different matter than allowing your system to accumulate bad debt that you will never collect. You may want to look at options such as payment plans rather than writing off outstanding balances.

Here are some simple additional steps you can take to uncover red flags in your billing department:

1. Take a look at your total monthly collection trend or simply the receipts being deposited in your bank account monthly for the past two years. If your work schedule and patient volumes have been steady, your receipts should be, too. Most practices will have some variance seasonally, so looking at a three or six month rolling average can even out short-term fluctuations. Declining collection trends warrant further investigation.

2. Review your gross collection percentage trend (collections divided by gross charges) over the past few years. A declining gross collection percentage, in absence of significant increases in your standard fee schedule, is an indication of either billing problems or declining reimbursement rates.

3. Review your accounts receivable aging trend. An accounts receivable aging is a listing of total balances outstanding by age, such as 0 to 30 days, 30 to 60 days, 60 to 90 days, etc. A trend of increasing balances in the 60-to-90 day and over-90 day categories means collections are falling behind. Balances over 90 days are generally not collectible.

Be wary of accounts receivable aging reports that look too perfect. Sometimes billing personnel or even practice managers will write off old balances to make the aging reports look good.

Reimbursement rates for both commercial payors and Medicare/Medicaid vary widely by geographic area. As discussed in Chapter 1, most small practices have little ability to negotiate with commercial payors. If your patient encounter volumes meet or exceed national standards, your coding is correct and there are no obvious problems in your billing department, it may be that your lower revenue is simply a reflection of low reimbursement. I urge caution here. Poor reimbursement is a common excuse used to mask poor billing and collections.

The sheer amount of billing data in a practice can make any review of reimbursement rates seem overwhelming. However, consider that in most practices the top 20 CPT® codes and three or four payors usually account for 80% to 90% of revenue.

Obtain and periodically review explanations of medical benefits (EOBs) from your top one or two payors, or have your office manager do so. Pay attention to what you are being paid for your most common CPT® codes. Compare these rates to what they were one and two years ago.

This doesn't have to be a major project. Ask to see a random EOB from one of your major commercial payors from a random month for each of the past three years. You will quickly see whether reimbursement rates are declining and what impact that is having on your revenue.

OVERHEAD AND OVERHEAD PERCENTAGE

If you have followed the above examination of revenue, you should have a pretty good idea of how your revenue compares to your peers and how it impacts your income. Now it is finally time to look at overhead. Most physicians want to look at overhead first, and while some practices do have bloated overhead, this is the exception rather than the rule.

You will need to determine your overhead percentage (overhead divided by revenue) and compare that to the MGMA survey. To do so, you will need to determine your "operating overhead."

Operating overhead doesn't include the salary and benefit costs of you or any other physician or mid-level provider in your practice. Nor does operating overhead include the physician discretionary expenses discussed above. The worksheet at the end of this chapter will help you determine your operating overhead to facilitate this comparison.

Regardless of what this comparison says, it is important to recognize that overhead percentage is the most misused statistic in medical practice management. A high overhead percentage compared to the MGMA survey does not necessarily mean your overhead is too high.

It is often overlooked that overhead percentage is the ratio of overhead to revenue. So revenue is a part of the equation as well. If you've completed the above analysis of your revenue and determined that your revenue is below average, you should already know that your overhead percentage is overstated. Your overhead percentage will magically go down when your revenue goes up. So don't jump to conclusions without looking objectively at both sides of the equation.

If your revenue is on par with national standards, then a high overhead percentage may indeed mean your overhead really is high. If this is the case, once again, you have to drill down.

In most practices, the largest component of overhead is in salaries and benefits. Take a look at your staffing levels per physician and compare them to the MGMA data. Review your salary levels and employee benefits. Many practices with low staff turnover find themselves with salary levels that are above prevailing market rates and find their benefits more generous than other practices in the area.

Take a look at what you're spending for drugs and supplies. A practice attitude that "company money" can be spent frivolously dramatically increases overhead.

TAKING ACTION

If you've found problems with your income, revenue, or overhead, you should begin to take corrective action before you go any further in pursuing the sale of your practice. As noted above, hospitals aren't interested in purchasing practices in need of a major turnaround, and selling at this point will likely result in a substandard financial arrangement for you, too. It is also unlikely that the sale of your practice will resolve many of the problems you have uncovered.

Your goal at this point should be to take the appropriate action to make your practice a stellar performer. This may require you to spend more time on business issues than you'd like, and it may require changes in policies, services, and personnel.

Preparing your practice for sale also means you need to step back and think in a broader strategic sense. There's an old adage that holds: "If you keep doing what you're doing, you'll keep getting what you're getting."

Strategically consider your practice's market position. Who is your competition and what are they doing? What can you do to improve your market share, volumes, visibility, and standing in the community? These are things that most small practices spend too little time thinking about, because the physicians are too busy seeing patients.

Don't overlook potential sources of revenue because of the overhead cost. For example, mid-level provider salaries are on the rise as demand for those services increases, but these professionals nationally generate a gross profit margin (that is, direct incremental revenue in excess of direct cost) equal to or in excess of the profit margin of a physician. Many practices still resist the opportunity to enhance their incomes using mid-level providers out of fear that their overhead will go up.

Mid-level providers offer practices a chance to increase provider capacity and market share without a huge long-term investment, and the return on that investment can be realized in 6 to 12 months. They don't expect to become partners in the practice, and their gross profit trickles down to bolster physician income and vastly enhance the value of your practice to a potential hospital purchaser.

If you already employ mid-level providers, look for ways to increase their productivity through better utilization. Consider extended office hours. Consider establishing disease management clinics staffed primarily by mid-level providers, for example, in diabetes care or management of lipids.

Make sure your practice is providing the full range of ancillary services for your specialty. I still see internal medicine groups without basic lab facilities and cardiology groups without nuclear capabilities. These services add significantly to the bottom line so important to maximizing your value with a hospital.

Stepping back and taking the time to understand your practice's performance will be invaluable whether you ultimately sell or not.

HOSPITAL PERSPECTIVE

Hospitals, especially those with experience in acquiring and employing physicians, are going to be more interested in well-run, financially growing practices. Hospitals with experience and expertise in managing physician practices will accept the challenges needed to turn around below average practices, but high-performing practices will be worth more and provide less acquisition risk to the hospital.

Despite what most physicians think, hospitals are more than willing to pay top dollar for well-run practices and top salaries to top-earning physicians, because these practices and physicians help them meet their business goals faster and with less effort.

Takeaway Points for Chapter 2

1. The biggest mistake physicians make in selling is that they jump in without adequate preparation. Planning ahead to make your business as attractive and as valuable as possible is a critical first step.
2. Step back and look at the real estate equivalent of curb appeal.
3. Don't fall into the trap of thinking you'll somehow be more attractive to a hospital suitor if you invest in state-of-the-art technology.
4. Your financial performance is the most important aspect of selling your practice. It will drive the value of your practice, your income post-sale, and maybe even the hospital's level of interest.
5. Your income is a driving factor behind the value of your practice and is a key aspect of your preparation to sell.
6. If your income is significantly below the MGMA median for your specialty in your geographic location, you need to find out why.
7. A vast majority of practices I have worked with over the past 20 years that have below-average physician incomes have that situation as the result of revenue issues.
8. Revenue trends declining even by only 1% or 2% per year can be construed as a declining practice.
9. Revenue is made up of several components and, if your revenue is below average, these should be examined individually: productivity, coding, billing and collections, and reimbursement rates.
10. While some practices do have bloated overhead, this is the exception rather than the rule.
11. Overhead percentage is the most misused statistic in medical practice management. A high overhead percentage does not necessarily mean your overhead is too high. Your overhead percentage will magically go down when your revenue goes up.
12. If you've found problems with your income, revenue, or overhead, you need to take corrective action before you go any further in pursuing the sale of your practice.
13. Preparing your practice for sale also means you need to step back and think in a broader strategic sense, perhaps looking for additional revenue streams.
14. Stepping back and taking the time to understand your practice's performance will be invaluable whether you sell or not.

Chapter 2 Checklist: How Pretty Is Your Practice?

Use this checklist to rate the curb appeal and staging of your practice, because these elements affect the potential purchaser's perception of your practice even if they don't affect the financial valuation. (This also affects patients' and potential patients' perceptions, too, of course.)

Physical Component	Rating (Good, Fair, Bad)	Notes for Improvement (If Needed)
Building exterior		
Building interior hallway and front door		
Condition of waiting room furniture: Is it welcoming and tidy?		
Condition of flooring?		
Reception desk: Is it easily identified and approachable by patients? Is the area relatively clutter free?		
Exam rooms: Attractive and adequately equipped?		
Physician offices: Do they reflect a well-managed practice?		
Equipment: Does it appear well-maintained even if older?		

Income/Overhead Percentage Worksheet	
A. Practice Revenue	
B. Physician and Provider Salaries, Benefits and Discretionary Expenses	
Physician owner salary or net income	
+ Associate physician salaries	
+ Mid-level provider salaries	
+ Provider payroll taxes	
+ Provider health, life, and disability insurance benefits	
+ Provider pension and profit sharing contributions	
+ Auto expense	
+ Continuing education	
+ Travel expense	
+ Meals and entertainment	
+ Other provider discretionary expenses	
B. Total Physician Provider Salaries and Benefits	
C. (A—B) = True Practice Overhead	
D. (C ÷ A) = True Practice Overhead Percentage	
E. Benchmark Overhead Percentage	

CHAPTER 3

Choosing the Right Hospital Partner

In choosing a partner, always pick the optimist.

TONY LEMA

Choosing the right hospital partner is key to a long-term successful relationship. All hospitals are not created equal when it comes to being physician-friendly and having a commitment to long-term success with practice acquisition and physician employment strategy. Hospitals that lack experience should be looked at with a healthy degree of skepticism.

HISTORICAL BACKGROUND

While hospitals are purchasing physician practices at a rate not seen since the 1990s and the action is widespread, this trend is not a repeat of the '90s. A short history lesson is in order. The '90s saw a feeding frenzy of hospitals snapping up physician practices. Bidding wars erupted in many areas of the country and prices were driven up as a result. This '90s trend toward integration was driven by two main factors: efforts at healthcare reform legislation and physician practice management companies.

The healthcare reform proposed by the Clinton administration had its underpinning in capitation and large integrated networks. Hospitals' acquisition of practices was initially driven by their desire to develop an adequate physician network.

Practice management companies were pioneered by Nashville-based PhyCor. Literally dozens of copycats followed fueled by Wall Street venture capital and public stock offerings. The model was really quite simple: they would offer the physicians a payment for their practice—usually in stock or a combination of stock and cash up front, in exchange for a long-term (30- to 40-year) management contract.

The practice management companies' entry into the physician acquisition market resulted in competition with hospitals and that further drove prices up.

Practice management companies didn't do a very good job of managing practices. Wall Street demanded growth to keep their stock prices up, and that growth was easier to fuel by acquiring more and larger practices than by actually managing those they had already acquired. The practices they had purchased became disenchanted by the high management fees and perceived lack of management and, in the end, sought termination of the management agreements. The growth needed to produce higher stock prices was unsustainable, and the whole practice management company industry came crashing down and virtually disappeared from the scene in a very short period of time.

Hospitals, for the most part, did an even worse job of managing physician practices. Hampered by long-term salary guarantees demanded by the physicians coupled with a lack of physician productivity standards, productivity fell by 20–25%.

Hospitals also often layered on corporate overhead, so their promises of reducing overhead often resulted in permanent increases instead. Many hospitals didn't invest in experienced physician practice professionals, physician billing systems, and financial controls. Many of the hospitals who did hire professionals dedicated those professionals to focus on acquiring more practices.

When the losses mounted, hospitals often responded by cutting staff in the practices, which further hampered efforts to stimulate productivity. Within a year or two, hospitals were losing an average of $100,000 per physician annually, and that didn't include the huge upfront investments they had made in acquiring practices. The acquisition binge became a divestiture binge. An implosion similar to that of the practice management companies took place. Long-time CEOs were dismissed, many hospitals had their debt ratings lowered, and some hospitals even had to be sold as a result of the huge losses sustained.

Physicians found themselves facing the reality that they had been overpaid and that their future incomes were going to be less. Many physicians' incomes never approached the levels they had under the cushy deals with hospitals.

Many physicians think the current trend is simply a repeat of those heady days of the 1990s. It is most assuredly not. The lessons from this debacle were learned. This time hospitals are approaching the business of acquiring and managing physician practices much differently. While there are many good reasons to sell your practice to a hospital, they do not include a big buyout and long-term salary guarantee.

HOSPITAL MOTIVATIONS

Hospitals, of course, aren't purchasing practices for altruistic reasons. While hospitals can't legally compel physicians they employ to use their facilities, the practical fact is you don't bite the hand that feeds you. Hospitals need physicians to maintain and grow market share, support service lines, and show third-party payors they have an extensive network of providers to serve their patient base.

In smaller, nonurban markets, hospitals can substantially grow market share by stopping out-migration of patients to larger urban hospitals by offering an expanded range of specialty services. Attracting specialty physicians to provide those services requires a robust primary care base to support those specialties, as well as hospital services such as diagnostic testing and surgeries.

Urban areas with intense hospital competition seek to make inroads into the competition's market share by expanding both their primary care and specialty physician base. They can do this by recruiting new physicians to the community or attracting the competing hospital's physicians with offers of employment and security.

HOSPITAL VIABILITY

At this initial stage, your goal should be to take an objective view of the hospital or hospitals you may be interested in joining. If they approach you, you should use this chapter to gain an understanding of their models, plans, and strategies for practice acquisition.

The first thing to do is to examine the business viability of the hospital you are considering. Ask for current financial statements and, if you don't understand them, work with your accountant to decipher the institution's financial picture.

If the hospital is independent, consider the likelihood of it being acquired or merging in the foreseeable future. Many hospitals operate on small margins and, while many still have deep pockets, the trend is toward being part of larger systems.

Hospitals that are part of larger systems are much more likely to invest in and maintain the practice management infrastructure necessary for successful practice management. The most important component of practice management infrastructure is personnel. Larger hospital systems are better at recruiting and retaining top level practice management professionals and, more importantly, giving them the autonomy to manage the practices.

Investment in technology—for things such as electronic medical records systems and state-of-the art practice management and billing systems—are critical, too. But remember, especially when dealing with hospitals inexperienced in acquiring physician practices, it is easy to throw money at technology. It is much more difficult to retain the professional management staff necessary to make that technology work.

QUESTIONS TO ASK

(Questions are repeated as a checklist at the end of this chapter)

While hospitals learned a lot from employing physicians in the 1990s, some didn't embody the lessons. Running a hospital department is different than running a physician practice. Make sure the hospital you choose has committed to or is willing to commit to the necessary investment in physician practice management infrastructure and expertise.

Hospitals should take a healthy, proactive approach to practice acquisition. Ask about their reasons for buying practices. The answers you are looking for include the following:

- Long-term strategy to grow or maintain market share
- Response to competitive threats
- Ability to better serve patients
- Increased leverage in negotiation with third-party payors
- Desire to help their medical staff members survive and thrive

Answers that should send up red flags might include the following:

- Our (hospital) competitors are buying practices
- We'll cut your overhead

Ask a lot of questions about the hospital's practice management commitment and be leery if you don't get specific answers:

1. How many physicians does the hospital currently employ?
2. How many practices do they plan to acquire?
3. What practice management expertise does the hospital currently have?
4. What practice management positions does the hospital anticipate adding in the future and/or what kind of background are they looking for to fill those positions?
5. How do they do, or plan to do, billing?
6. Will billing be a centralized function or will each practice keep its existing billing system?
7. Do they currently use or have plans for an EMR system?
8. Who will actually negotiate managed care contracts?

9. What is the hospital's business plan for practice acquisition and management?
10. How does my practice fit into that plan?

Talk to those physicians who have already gone through the acquisition process and ask:

1. How was it handled?
2. Are they happy?
3. Has the hospital been willing to work with them to resolve problems and issues?

Don't be afraid to ask questions specific to your situation.

1. Will you have a say in the hiring and termination of staff?
2. How will staff work rules be enforced?
3. Will you have input into staff evaluations, raises, and bonuses?
4. Can your office be moved or consolidated with another office without your approval?

While some details will have to be worked out in the future and things will evolve as the number of physicians they employ grows, "we'll figure that out later" as the answer to most of your questions should be a red flag as to how well the hospital has thought through its strategy.

Consider your past relationships with the hospital:

1. Is the hospital part of a larger system that has the financial resources necessary to assure long-term stability?
2. Is administration stable and trusted?
3. Do you look up to members of the management team as good leaders and role models?
4. Who will be your liaison?
5. Are the individuals in charge experienced and competent?
6. Are they honest and forthright in their business dealings?

Another consideration is how you would feel about answering to hospital administration. If you have had conflicts with administration in the past, you'll have to decide if you can put those behind you and work in close partnership moving forward.

Remember, too, that even if you have a rosy relationship with the hospital CEO and others, turnover at the executive level in hospitals tends to be fairly active. There is no guarantee that the people you deal with today will be in their positions a few years from now. Given that possibility, make sure all points of your agreement are in writing. What he or she said way back when matters little if a whole new team takes over the executive suite.

Ask yourself what the hospital has to offer that will improve the quality of your professional and/or personal life. Then consider if what it is offering is enough for you to give up your autonomy. An attractive buyout price, a solid compensation and benefit package, fewer administrative hassles, and more time for direct patient care might align quite well with your long-term career values and goals.

Understanding a hospital's motivation and strategy, along with its commitment to practice management infrastructure, is key in choosing the right hospital partner. It is not the hospital with the best offer that is likely to sustain you should you decide to sell—it is the hospital with the commitment to practice management infrastructure, a solid business plan, and the successful execution of that plan.

Takeaway Points for Chapter 3

1. Choosing the right hospital partner is key to a long-term successful relationship.
2. All hospitals are not created equal when it comes to being physician-friendly and having the commitment to a long-term strategy for successful practice acquisition and physician employment.
3. Hospitals that lack experience should be looked at with a healthy degree of skepticism.
4. While hospitals are purchasing physician practices at a rate not seen since the 1990s and the action is widespread, this trend is not a repeat of the '90s.
5. While there are many good reasons to sell your practice to a hospital, they do not include a big buyout and long-term salary guarantee.
6. Hospitals aren't purchasing practices for altogether altruistic reasons. They need physicians to maintain and grow market share, support service lines, and show third-party payors they have an extensive network of providers to serve their patient base.
7. Take a close look at the business viability of the hospital you are considering joining.
8. Make sure the hospital you choose is committed to making the necessary investment in physician practice management infrastructure and expertise.
9. Ask a lot of questions and be leery if you don't get straight answers. "We'll figure that out later" as the answer to most of your questions should be a red flag as to how well the hospital has thought through its strategy.
10. Consider how you would feel about answering to hospital administration.

11. Ask yourself what the hospital has to offer that will improve the quality of your professional and/or personal life. Then consider if what it is offering is enough for you to give up your autonomy. An attractive buyout price, a solid compensation and benefit package, fewer administrative hassles, and more time for direct patient care might align quite well with your long-term career values and goals.

12. It is not the hospital with the best offer that is likely to sustain you should you decide to sell—it is the hospital with the commitment to practice management infrastructure, a solid business plan, and the successful execution of that plan.

Chapter 3 Checklist: Initial Questions for the Hospital and Employed Physicians

❏ A hospital should take a healthy, proactive approach to practice acquisition. Ask about its reasons for buying practices. The answers you are looking for include the following:
- Long-term strategy to grow or maintain market share
- Response to competitive threats
- Ability to better serve patients
- Increased leverage in negotiation with third-party payors
- Desire to help its medical staff members survive and thrive

❏ Answers that should send up red flags might include the following:
- Our (hospital) competitors are buying practices
- We'll cut your overhead

❏ Ask a lot of questions about the hospital's practice management commitment and be leery if you don't get specific answers:
- How many physicians does the hospital currently employ?
- How many practices does it plan to acquire?
- What practice management expertise does the hospital currently have?
- What practice management positions does the hospital anticipate adding in the future and/or what kind of background is it looking for to fill those positions?
- How does it do, or plan to do, billing?
- Will billing be a centralized function or will each practice keep its existing billing system?
- Does it currently use or have plans for an EMR system?
- Who will actually negotiate managed care contracts?
- What is the hospital's business plan for practice acquisition and management?
- How does my practice fit into that plan?
- Will I have a say in the hiring and termination of staff?
- How will staff work rules be enforced?
- Will I have input into staff evaluations, raises, and bonuses?
- Can my office be moved or consolidated with another office without my approval?

❏ Talk to physicians who have already gone through the acquisition process and ask these questions:
- How was it handled?
- Are they happy?
- Has the hospital been willing to work with them to resolve problems and issues?

CHAPTER 4

Valuation—What Is Your Practice Worth?

Until you value yourself, you won't value your time. Until you value your time, you will not do anything with it.   M. SCOTT PECK

If you decide to further explore the sale of your practice and see what your chosen hospital has to offer, the hospital will engage an independent firm—chosen and paid for by the hospital—to assess your practice and arrive at a fair market value.

You will be asked to share extensive financial and operating data. Providing complete and accurate data is important. Incomplete documentation tends to reduce the value of a practice because, absent documentation, the valuation firm is likely to make the most conservative assumptions. This is where the efforts you took in preparing your practice in Chapter 2 will start to pay off.

VALUATION COMPONENTS

The value of any business, including physician practices, generally consists of two types of assets: tangible and intangible.

Tangible assets in a physician practice consist of furniture and equipment, inventory and supplies, and accounts receivable. Many practices also own the practice's facility, often through a separate real estate entity that leases the facility to the practice.

Intangible assets include things like an established patient base, reputation of the physician(s), an established referral base, a trained workforce, patient medical records, and the name and phone number of the practice. Intangible assets are often referred to as "goodwill."

A valuation worksheet is provided at the end of this chapter to assist you in estimating the value of your practice for comparison to the hospital's valuation.

VALUATION OF TANGIBLE ASSETS

The valuation of tangible assets and how they are handled in a hospital sale are fairly standard. Furniture and equipment will be valued less than your original cost but probably more than their current net book value for tax purposes. Net book value is simply the original cost less the total depreciation you have been allowed to deduct on your tax return since you purchased the asset.

Tax law generally allows depreciating assets over a fairly short period of time—generally a much shorter time than the actual period the asset will be used in the practice—net book value is generally going to understate the actual value of your furniture and equipment.

Most appraisers will use a method that values the assets based on their age, original cost, and the period they are likely to be in actual use in the practice. The appraiser will likely ask for a copy of a work paper your CPA firm maintains for use in preparation of your tax return called a depreciation schedule. A depreciation schedule lists all the assets purchased by your practice over the years, including a description, date acquired, and original cost.

Depreciation schedules are often incomplete and out of date. Make sure you review yours and that it is up to date and complete. If not, you will want to discuss this with the appraisers as they, too, will want accurate and complete information.

Another method that is sometimes used is replacement cost. The appraiser will estimate the replacement cost of furnishing a physician office with equipment of like utility and then value your assets at a percentage of replacement cost based on the age and condition of your equipment.

A rule of thumb that can be used to estimate the value of a practice's furniture and equipment is to take net book value and add back 50% of the accumulated depreciation shown on your balance sheet. Your CPA can help you with this calculation if necessary or you can try it yourself utilizing the worksheet at the end of this chapter. While this method will not be totally accurate, it will give you a rough idea of the value to expect.

Make sure you exclude from your estimate assets that tend to be more personal in nature. The hospital likely isn't interested in purchasing any antique furniture, original artwork, and practice-owned vehicles.

Finally, be sure to disclose equipment that is in need of repairs, even though it may be tempting to avoid doing so. You don't want to get your relationship with your new hospital partners off to a bad start over a small issue with equipment. The belief you were deliberately misleading them in the sales process could quickly be construed that you will mislead the hospital on other issues as well.

Accounts receivable (A/R) represents work you've already done and, while a tangible asset of your practice, is usually not part of the transaction. If a hospital does purchase A/R, it will do so at a discounted rate and then attempt to collect (and keep) what it gets post-sale. In most instances, it's better for both parties if the physician keeps the outstanding A/R. Hospitals will usually allow your billing staff, who become their employees after the sale, to spend some time each week for a few months collecting your A/R.

Inventory and supplies generally are not a significant component of the tangible value. If you have an extensive inventory of drugs and supplies, it will be to your benefit to provide copies of recent invoices to aid the hospital in assigning a fair value to these items. Don't attempt to enhance your value by trying to sell expired vaccines and drugs at full price: the hit on your reputation and future relationships are not worth the few extra dollars gained.

If you own your office building, it generally will be owned in an entity separate from your practice entity. Many hospitals will not purchase physician-owned real estate. Instead, the hospital will enter into a space lease for the office at a fair market value rental rate. If this is the hospital's approach, be sure the lease terms are adequate and there is clear agreement on things like taxes, insurance, repairs, and maintenance.

Many physicians desire to sell their real estate with the practice. Some hospitals will purchase real estate, especially if it is located in a desirable location. Here, too, the hospital will engage an independent third-party appraiser (often a different appraiser than the one who valued the practice) and will be bound by their valuation. If you don't feel the appraisal reflects the fair value of the facility, consider leasing it to the hospital for a few years and then have the property reappraised. Another option is to sell your real estate to a third-party investor or real estate developer.

VALUATION OF INTANGIBLE ASSETS

The value of tangible assets, with the exception of real estate, usually does not represent the bulk of what a physician thinks the practice is worth. Most physicians have the expectation of value in the intangible assets or what is commonly known as goodwill.

Physicians tend to think their practices are worth more than they actually are. The first argument is usually how much revenue the practice generates for the hospital by admitting patients and making referrals for diagnostic testing and therapeutic care. This is an easy one to set aside: It is illegal for a hospital to factor this in, and no reputable hospital would do so.

The second argument is that there has to be value in the practice's goodwill. After all, returning patients, the reputation of the doctors, an established referral base, medical records, and even the name and phone number of the practice are what make the practice a viable business, so those things have to have value.

While this goodwill does exist, the reality is that in the sale of a practice, it often has little or no value. This is because the value of almost any business is in the future earnings stream that the business can be expected to generate for its owner. In this case, the owner will be the hospital. If the earnings stream the practice generates for the hospital is paid out to the physicians in salary and bonus, as it generally is, then there is no earnings stream to base the value on.

Another way to think of this is that you are, in effect, benefiting from the goodwill of the practice each year through the earnings it generates for you.

Most valuation firms will value your practice based on what is called the discounted cash flow (DCF) method, which is the preferred method of valuation. While the name may sound complex, the DCF method is really quite simple.

The appraiser will develop a projection of the future financial performance of the practice, usually for a period of five years. This financial projection consists of three key components: revenue, practice overhead, and provider compensation.

Any projected future earnings are discounted to the present to arrive at the value; hence the term "discounted" cash flow. The discount simply reflects the time value of money (because a dollar in the future is worth less in today's dollars) and the risk inherent in attaining the future projected cash flow. The resulting number or DCF value represents what is often referred to as the business enterprise value or total value of the practice.

The value of the goodwill is simply the excess of this business enterprise value over and above the value of the tangible assets of the practice. The valuation worksheet at the end of this chapter should help you understand the relationships and how they will impact the value of your practice.

This is where your revenue and overhead are normalized based on your practice's historical performance and current situation. The hospital won't pay you in upfront value for improvements they plan to make to improve the performance of the practice, such as better billing and collections, payor contracts, or overhead reductions. You will want to make sure that your incentive compensation (see Chapter 5) doesn't penalize you if the changes they implement don't work out and result in decreased revenue, increased overhead, and decreased earnings.

MAXIMIZING YOUR VALUE

The DCF method is why demonstrating a healthy financial picture is important. Showing a healthy annual increase in revenue for the past year or two will support projecting a higher rate of revenue growth in the future. This may translate into a higher revenue projection that could result in a higher earnings stream and DCF value. Conversely, historical overhead that increases at stable or low rates will support lower expense projections.

Regardless of the projections, provider compensation makes or breaks a practice valuation. Historically, the earnings stream in almost all medical practices is paid out to the owners of the practice in the form of salary and bonuses. If the financial projections assume the physicians continue to be paid virtually 100% of the funds available after overhead, there will be no value for the practice beyond the value of the furniture, fixtures, and equipment.

The physician compensation used in the valuation model will likely be based on the median compensation for physicians in your specialty based on either the MGMA surveys or one of the other resources discussed in Chapter 2. If your historical compensation is less than those of your peers, the practice will likely have no projected earnings and therefore no value beyond the value of the furniture, fixtures, and equipment. This is why you want your historical income to be above average and why the steps in Chapter 2 are so important.

While the prospect that your practice may have no goodwill value may be surprising and disappointing, if you step back and think about it, it makes sense. Why would anyone purchase a practice without a reasonable expectation of generating a profit from its operation? As noted above, the hospital cannot consider the value of any referrals because that would squarely be at odds with federal law.

So if you want to maintain your current income *and* get a big price for your practice, prepare to be disappointed. *Continuing 100% of your historical earnings post-acquisition will leave no future earnings for the value to be based on, in which case there will be no value beyond the value of your hard assets.*

If the compensation you ultimately negotiate (Chapter 5) is higher than the compensation used in the DCF model to value your practice, the value of your practice may actually go down. Most hospitals and valuation firms require that the DCF model accurately reflect the compensation that will be paid to the physician post-sale, including an estimate of incentive compensation. So the valuation model is often recalculated based on the agreed-upon salary and incentive structure, and the value will go up or down as a result. *This is the inverse relationship between practice value and post-sale compensation—higher salary equals lower value and lower salary equals higher value.*

It is possible to increase the value of your practice by agreeing to put a portion of your compensation at risk, that is, by agreeing to a lower salary. For example, you may agree to a salary of $25,000 less per year. The result will be an increase in the earnings stream of $25,000 per year in the DCF projection model, which may lead to a higher practice value.

This may sound like a good deal, but generally it is not. Your base salary will generally be locked in at the lower level for five years, and this salary is usually not guaranteed because it will be subject to productivity standards (see Chapter 5). As noted above, any incentive compensation has to be estimated and included in the valuation model as well. There are tax implications that may need to be considered, too. So while some hospitals may consider this model, at the end of the day most hospitals will shy away from such a structure because they don't want to be paying huge upfront values.

Entire books have been written on valuing physician practices. Practice brokers and dozens of firms are on the Internet offering, for a price or commission, to tell you what your practice is worth and to help you sell it. If you are going to sell to a hospital, don't bother. It doesn't matter what these firms tell you. The hospital is going to be bound by the value determined by its independent appraiser and no more.

Many hospitals, both for-profit and not-for-profit, are taking an even more conservative approach: They simply have a policy against paying for goodwill—period. In many areas of the country, physicians are approaching hospitals—which indicates that in these areas there is a buyer's market. In a buyer's market, there is no compelling reason to pay for goodwill regardless of the practice's value.

Even in areas where there is competition between hospitals for practices, CEOs and hospital board members remember the lessons from the '90s. Many simply are not willing to expose their hospital (or their job security) to repeating past mistakes.

The only way to get a better value for your practice is to properly prepare your practice for sale (Chapter 2) and focus on the things that matter: a demonstrated ability to earn well above the regional average for your specialty, a solid history of revenue growth, and a willingness to put part of your historical compensation at risk based on the future performance of the practice.

ANCILLARY SERVICES

Practices that provide ancillary services often desire to treat these services as a separate business during the valuation process. Their argument is that if the provision of, for example, CT scans through an imaging center is generating a profit, that earnings stream has a separate and discrete value.

While ancillary services can generate a significant profit for a physician practice, many physicians tend to overstate the income they generate. Ancillary services provided through the physician practice are essentially operating as a department within the practice.

The nature of practice accounting systems is that the "profit" generated doesn't fully reflect the cost of operating the ancillary service. Scheduling and billing are two common examples of services that are generally provided by the practice but whose costs are not separately allocated and reflected in internal financial reports. So that CT scanner's profit would be significantly less if it were truly a stand-alone business.

An even more significant issue in valuing in-office ancillary services is one the physicians often forget: *The ancillary profits, however they are calculated, are already reflected in physician incomes from the practice and are therefore already reflected in the practice's valuation.*

Physicians seeking to maintain their current income post-sale and get a separate buy-out for their CT business are double-dipping. Their incomes already include profits from the CT. Therefore, that earnings stream has no value to the hospital purchaser, because the physician is already taking the profits as part of his or her compensation.

HOSPITAL PERSPECTIVE

In spite of what physicians assume, the hospital likely isn't trying to lowball you on the value of your practice or in your post-sale compensation. Many hospitals are willing to pay the full value of your practice as determined by the outside independent valuation firm. They are not willing to overpay for your practice, because that would be illegal. As noted above, an increasing number of hospitals simply are not willing to pay for goodwill value, regardless of the valuation, as a matter of policy.

The hospital wants you to be financially successful post-sale. They want you to be happy and don't care if your income increases substantially as long as they don't have significant losses on your practice. This almost universal unwillingness to lose money on employing physicians is largely a result of their experiences in the '90s and, for better or worse, reflects the current state of the market.

Takeaway Points for Chapter 4

1. The hospital will engage an independent firm, chosen and paid for by the hospital, to assess your practice and to arrive at a fair market value.
2. Providing complete and accurate data is important. Absent documentation, the valuation firm is likely to make the most conservative assumptions.
3. Physicians tend to think their practices are worth more than they actually are.
4. The value of any business generally consists of two types of assets: tangible and intangible.
5. Tangible assets consist of furniture and equipment, inventory and supplies, and accounts receivable.
6. Intangible assets include things like an established patient base, reputation of the physician(s), an established referral base, patient medical records, and the name and phone number of the practice. Intangible assets are often referred to as goodwill.
7. The valuation of tangible assets and how they are handled in a hospital sale are fairly standard. Furniture and equipment will be valued less than your original cost but probably more than their current net book value.
8. Usually the physician will keep the outstanding A/R, and the hospital will allow your billing staff to collect it post-sale.
9. Many hospitals will not purchase physician-owned real estate. Instead the hospital will enter into a space lease at fair market value rental rates. Be sure the lease terms are adequate and there is clear agreement on things like taxes, insurance, repairs, and maintenance.
10. Most physicians have the expectation of value in the intangible assets or what is commonly known as goodwill. The reality is that in the sale of a practice goodwill often has little or no value.
11. If the earnings stream the practice generates for the hospital is paid out to the physicians in salary and bonus, then there is no earnings stream for the hospital and little value in the business beyond the tangible assets.
12. Showing a healthy annual increase in revenue could result in a higher value.
13. If you want to maintain your current income and get a big price for your practice, prepare to be disappointed.

14. Ancillary profits are already reflected in physician incomes and, therefore, are already reflected in the practice's valuation.

15. Many hospitals are willing to pay the full value for your practice and don't care how much you earn. What they are unwilling to do is to lose significant money on employing physicians.

16. An increasing number of hospitals simply are not willing to pay for goodwill value, regardless of the valuation, as a matter of policy.

PRACTICE VALUATION WORKSHEET

The purpose of this worksheet is to provide a simple tool for estimating the value of your practice. These are estimates only and will likely vary from the hospital's valuation. This worksheet should be used to highlight differences between the actual value of your practice and your estimate and as an aid in raising questions for discussion with the hospital.

Furniture, Fixtures and Equipment (FF&E)	Practice Estimate	Hospital Value
Cost		
– Accumulated depreciation		
= Net book value		
+ 50% of Accumulated depreciation		
= Estimated Value of FF&E		

Accounts Receivable	Practice Estimate	Hospital Value
Accounts receivable outstanding less than 60 days		
– Practice's gross collection percentage (See Chapter 2 for definition)		
= Estimated Value of Accounts Receivable		

Inventory and Supplies	Practice Estimate	Hospital Value
Office supplies expense last year		
+ Medical supplies expense last year		
+ Vaccine and drug expense last year		
= Total Drug and supply expense		
× Total by .1667 = Estimated Value		

Business Enterprise or Total Practice Value	Practice Estimate	Hospital Value
Practice revenue last year		
– True practice overhead last year (see Chapter 2 worksheet)		
– Post-sale provider compensation × 1.15 (including employed and mid-level providers)		
= Practice earnings		
× Practice Earnings by 4 = Total Estimated Practice Value		

Practice Value Summary	Practice Estimate	Hospital Value
Total Estimated Practice Value		
– Estimated Value of FF&E		
– Estimated Value of Accounts Receivable		
× Estimated Value of Inventory and Supplies		
= Goodwill Value (if negative number, goodwill value is zero)		

CHAPTER 5

Deal Structure

Hospital acquisition of a physician practice generally consists of two components: an asset purchase agreement and an employment agreement.
In some situations there may be other agreements. For example, if real
estate is being purchased, this would be subject to a separate real estate purchase
agreement.

ASSET PURCHASE AGREEMENT

The asset purchase agreement is simply an agreement wherein you agree to sell and
the hospital agrees to purchase specified practice assets for a specified price with
specified payment terms.

The assets included will vary but generally include all of the tangible furniture,
fixtures, and equipment along with your inventory and supplies. Asset purchase
agreements also generally include intangible assets such as the practice's name,
phone number, and patient records, even if a separate value is not being assigned
to these items.

Many physicians question why they should agree to sell these items for little
or no value. The answer is that these intangible assets are part of the practice and
most hospitals are going to insist on including them. You may choose to think of
this as the cost of getting the hospital to enter into the employment agreement
discussed below.

Asset purchase agreements are usually pretty straightforward. You will attest you
own the assets being sold and that they are free of liens and encumbrances. There will
generally be a list of the assets. Review this listing carefully and make sure any personal items, which are often present in physician offices, are excluded from the sale.

Any debt your practice has outstanding, including loans to purchase equipment
or any loans secured by your practice's assets, will generally not be assumed by the
hospital. You will likely need to make arrangements to pay these loans off and get
any security interests released prior to closing.

Equipment and space leases will likely be assumed by the hospital. Generally the
permission of the equipment leasing company and your landlord will need to be

secured prior to closing as well. While seeking such approvals is often considered a formality, it is possible for these details to delay closing, so it is best to identify these issues to the hospital in advance so their legal counsel can be working on getting the necessary paperwork completed.

Asset purchase agreements often also will include a restrictive covenant or non-compete provision as well. These are discussed in detail below.

While you never want to plan for failure, consider whether you want a provision that states how you will purchase the assets back in the future. Sometimes the security of knowing how the assets will be revalued at some future date is comforting. Other times you may be better off just leaving this to chance—after all, if the deal fails, the hospital may not want your old equipment and you might get a better deal if the price or valuation method isn't stated.

EMPLOYMENT AGREEMENT

The employment agreement is your agreement to become an employee of the hospital and will set out the employment terms, the termination provisions, and the all-important compensation provisions including salary, incentive compensation, and benefits.

The employment agreement is generally much more important than the asset purchase agreement. The employment agreement will specify both parties' rights and obligations and otherwise govern your day-to-day work from now on. Make sure you fully understand its provisions. The employment agreement also should be given a detailed review by your attorney, who may raise additional questions and issues.

The following are some key provisions you will want to understand:

Compensation

Base salary and incentive compensation post-sale are by far the most important financial aspects of selling your practice. If you have chosen your potential hospital partner wisely, you should have every expectation that your practice income will stabilize or even increase.

This is an area where you can't ask too many questions and where involvement of your CPA or practice advisor is highly recommended. Compensation plans can be quite complex and you want to be sure to understand where the numbers come from and how the calculations are made. Don't be afraid to ask for examples and language clarifications. Insist on sample illustrations of incentive compensation calculations.

Base salary and productivity standards

The employment agreement will typically provide for a base salary. This base salary is likely based on your historical earnings. As discussed in Chapter 2, you will want to make sure the historical earnings actually reflect the earning potential of the practice and that your historical income has been adjusted for physician discretionary expenses.

Base salary is often negotiable but, remember, a higher base salary may result in a downward adjustment in the value of your practice in certain situations because of that inverse relationship between practice value and compensation discussed in Chapter 4.

Sometimes the base salary is guaranteed for a period of time, usually no longer than one or two years. This period can sometimes be negotiated as well, but most employment contracts will still require some level of productivity be maintained to earn the base salary. These productivity standards are almost a universal part of post-'90s physician employment contracts, because hospitals saw physician productivity plummet 20–25% under the guaranteed salary employment contracts that were so prevalent in the '90s.

Productivity standards come in many variations, and understanding how they were determined and how they will be calculated in the future is critical. The typical contract will offer you a base salary that is contingent on maintaining a specified productivity standard similar to what you have produced historically.

For example, if you had 3,000 patient encounters last year, the standard may be that you agree to maintain patient encounters of no less than 90%—or 2,700 patient encounters—to earn your base salary. If encounters fall below that number, there may be a prorated reduction in your base salary. So if your base salary is, for example, $150,000 and your patient encounters drop by 10%, your base salary may drop by 10% to $135,000.

Regardless of the productivity standard used, you will want to be sure the definition of the standard is included in the contract language and that the definition is consistent with how your historical data was used to calculate the standard. In other words, make sure the productivity standard is calculated the same way on the front end and the back end.

Some of the more common productivity standards and some of their pitfalls are described below:

Patient encounters are the most basic productivity standard. The main pitfalls with patient encounter thresholds are defining an encounter and the accuracy of the historical patient encounter data from which the standard is derived.

Physician billing systems often do not provide ready access to encounter data and such data often has to be manually extracted by CPT® code. There are also varying definitions of what exactly constitutes a patient encounter.

For example, does the data include encounters of a mid-level provider that were billed incident-to under the physician's name? What about nursing-only visits or rechecks that are billed under the physician's name? Practices handle these issues in varying ways. Finding that one definition was used in developing the standard and then another one is used by the hospital in evaluating the standard post-sale will result in problems down the road. It will always be beneficial to deal with these detail-type issues up front to avoid problems later.

Sometimes, especially in cases where mid-level provider visits are billed incident-to under a physician's name, accurate encounter data is simply not available. In this case, it may be necessary to manually determine encounters from an appointment schedule or log or agree to utilize a different standard.

Gross charges are another common productivity standard. Gross charges are a fair reflection of physician work effort from year to year only so long as the fee schedule on which they are based is consistent. Many practices are lax in updating their fee schedules. Hospitals, especially those experienced in practice management, will typically update fee schedules regularly based on national or regional norms.

Relative value units, or RVUs, are increasingly used as a productivity standard. RVUs are essentially a measure of the relative work, training, and expertise needed to provide a medical service. They form the basis for the Medicare physician fee schedule on which Medicare and most commercial payors base their reimbursement rates.

RVUs, by their nature, reflect physician coding. Two physicians seeing the same patient for the same problem can and do code differently. This difference is often a reflection of documentation. So it is possible for two physicians, working equally as hard and seeing the same number of patients with the same acuity, to have varying levels of RVUs.

If you completed the steps in preparing your practice for sale in Chapter 2, hopefully you reviewed your coding and documentation. RVU productivity standards are another place where accurate coding is important.

As with patient encounters, many physician billing systems do not provide RVU data and such data often has to be manually calculated. In addition, RVUs can and do change, and billing systems that provide this data often use outdated RVU values. This raises two issues:

1. You want to be sure the RVU data your productivity standard is based on is accurate.
2. Since RVU values will likely change in the future, you will want to make sure you understand how your productivity standard will be adjusted to reflect these future changes.

Cash collection productivity standards

Some hospitals, especially those with little or no experience in the employment of physicians, will seek to minimize downside risk by attempting to measure productivity based on collections. Depending on how billing and collection functions are handled post-sale, this introduces a variable into the equation that you may not be able to control—the hospital's ability to bill and collect.

Using cash collections as a productivity standard could have an upside for physicians as well because, if the hospital does a better job of billing and collection or has better payor contracts, the physician will realize the benefit without any additional effort.

Hospitals with successful experience in practice management tend to have billing and collection down to an art. They often have invested heavily in technology, systems, and experienced personnel and have top-tier billing offices. The trick is figuring out if your chosen hospital knows what it is doing before you agree to a cash collection productivity standard.

Incentive compensation

Incentive compensation is one of the most important components of your post-sale employment. It also can be one of the most complex. Carefully consider what type of incentive is right for you given your practice style and current situation.

While all hospitals are prohibited from paying physicians for referrals, not-for-profit hospitals must also contend with the issue of their tax-exempt status. As a result, not-for-profit hospitals generally have more complex physician incentive plans.

Simply stated, not-for-profit hospitals cannot inure benefits to private individuals. Compensation levels for individuals are required to be reasonable and "excess compensation" is prohibited. Some not-for-profit hospitals get around these restrictions by establishing for-profit subsidiaries to employ physicians, but this is not always possible. If a for-profit subsidiary is not used, most not-for-profit hospital legal counsels will insist compensation be subject to a cap.

There are other related complexities as well. The Stark Law and its associated regulations make it difficult or impossible in some situations for profits from most ancillary services, such as lab and imaging, to be part of physician incentive compensation.

These profits cannot be distributed directly to the physician ordering the tests, regardless of whether the services are provided in private practice or under hospital employment. The profits from these services have to be pooled and allocated to individual physicians in a method that is not directly or indirectly related to the volume or value of referrals. In a hospital employment arrangement, especially with not-for-profit hospitals, there may be other restrictions as well.

The following describes some of the more common incentive compensation plans:

Profit-based incentives have become the most common type of incentive plan because they, by their very nature, protect hospitals from losing money on physician practices. Profit-based incentives don't prevent hospitals from losing money but, without profits, hospitals aren't obligated to pay incentive compensation, which limits their downside.

Profit-based incentives are generally not available for use by not-for-profit hospitals unless a for-profit subsidiary can be established. Even in that case, hospital legal counsel will often insist compensation be subject to a cap.

Hospitals make profit-based incentive plans attractive, because they protect the hospital's downside. Hospitals will typically offer a high percentage of profits to the physicians: 50% is typical, but I've see the incentive percentage go as high as 90%.

The key issue with these profit-based incentive plans is in the definition of profits. Is revenue based on cash collections? If so, the ability of the hospital to bill and collect has to be considered, as discussed above.

Does overhead include an allocation for the hospital's management infrastructure and such things as accounting, payroll processing, billing, and administration? While allocation of direct costs is reasonable, some hospitals, especially those inexperienced in practice management, will allocate administrative overhead and other costs well in excess of the fair value of the services provided.

Some hospitals will attempt to allocate the depreciation and amortization of the purchase price paid for the practice. While allocation of depreciation expense on tangible assets is reasonable, allocating the amortization of goodwill (in instances where it exists) virtually assures ongoing operating losses.

Profit-based incentives can be lucrative to physicians, and they are effective in aligning incentives between the physicians and the hospital.

Productivity-based incentives are another common type of incentive program. Simply stated, incentive compensation is based on a sharing of productivity in excess of a preestablished threshold.

Productivity-based incentives are structured in the same ways as productivity standards discussed above: They are based on either patient encounters, gross charges, RVUs, or cash collections. The same caveats apply as well: Be sure the definition of the productivity incentive is included in the contract language and that the definition is consistent with your historical data.

The weakness of a productivity-based incentive from the hospital perspective is that it provides no incentive for the physicians to control costs. Physicians can earn huge incentives while the hospital can incur huge operating losses.

Enterprise incentives are more typically used by not-for-profit hospitals that cannot establish a for-profit subsidiary and seek a way to provide an effective incentive plan within the confines of their not-for-profit structure.

These plans tend to be complex, but they generally seek to establish an incentive based on the hospital's employed physicians, as a group, attaining certain financial and operational goals. While these plans can be very lucrative, they effectively put incentive compensation out of the direct control of individual physicians and rely instead on broader goals and group-wide objectives.

Ask a lot of questions if such a proposal is made, and ask to see sample—or even actual—calculations in cases where the incentive has been in use with other practices. Ask how the incentive has been realized in the past. Talk to other physicians who have operated under the plan to gauge their satisfaction. These types of plans tend to be frustrating to high performing physicians, because they can be penalized for the inability of others to contribute to the team effort.

Termination with cause

Most employment agreements provide for termination with cause. Cause is usually defined to include such things as death, disability, conviction of a felony, etc. While some of these causes are easy to recognize, care needs to be taken where the determination is vague. For example, what is the definition of disability? How is it determined? Is there an appeal process?

Termination without cause

Sometimes both sides have done everything right and it just doesn't work. Other times, unanticipated issues come up and the parties need to compromise. Some hospitals, seeking to avoid these conflicts, are offering termination without cause provisions. These provisions generally provide that either party, on giving required notice (usually 90 to 180 days) can terminate the relationship for any reason.

Termination-without-cause provisions often have the opposite effect: Rather than resulting in hasty terminations, they provide the parties a pathway to work together in resolving issues and strengthening the relationship. Since the termination option is mutual, both sides have equal leverage if the financial or other terms are not acceptable. This tends to aid in reaching necessary compromises.

The termination provisions will generally state the required notice and the financial aspects of the unwinding of the transaction. You will want to understand the financial and legal implications of either party exercising the termination option. It is a double-edged sword—while you can get out if it's not working from your perspective, you can also be forced out if it's not working from the hospital's perspective.

How will you purchase your practice back? How will the price be determined and under what terms will you be required to make payment? How will malpractice tail coverage be handled? Will the restrictive covenant be waived? There are many details.

Finally, make sure an adequate notice time is provided for in the contract. While 180 days may seem like an eternity, once you've made the decision to go back on your own, you will likely need much of that time to get your provider numbers and payor contracts back in your name, reestablish billing and collections functions, transition staff back to your employment, and get the legal documentation completed.

Restrictive covenant (non-compete)

Most employment agreements (and some asset purchase agreements as noted above) are going to include some kind of restrictive covenant or non-compete provision. Restrictive covenants generally prohibit you from practicing medicine for a specified period of time within a specified distance of a geographic location such as the hospital or your office location.

While the idea of a restrictive covenant may seem offensive, absent a non-compete provision, your practice has no value to the hospital.

You will want to make sure the time, distance, and geographic location parameters of the non-compete are reasonable and practical. For example, a non-compete that restricts you from practicing within 20 miles of your practice location is less restrictive than one that prohibits you from practicing within 20 miles of any hospital-owned practice location.

These time, distance, and geographic location parameters are often negotiable and need to be considered in the context of your practice's service area, demographics, and competitive environment. These issues need to be considered carefully because you may be putting your future ability to practice in the area at risk if it doesn't work out.

The enforceability and reasonableness of restrictive covenants are subject to state law and often complex legal precedents. Restrictive covenants are not enforceable in some states and other states limit their enforceability to specific circumstances. Legal counsel with specific experience in this area should be consulted.

Finally, you will want to relate the non-compete to the termination provisions. Generally the non-compete should not apply if the contract is terminated for breach by the hospital, or termination by either party without cause (if the contract provides for such termination), or if the contract expires without renewal.

Retention bonuses

Some hospitals offer future incentive payments to induce physicians to sell. These usually take the form of retention bonuses. Retention bonuses come in many variations. For example, sometimes the hospital will agree to pay a specified dollar amount on the anniversary date of your employment for several years. Sometimes a certain percentage of your revenue, compensation, or bonus is set aside annually and paid in a lump sum after a specified period of time.

Retention bonuses generally are not prorated or paid in the event of early termination but, to the extent the hospital terminates the contract early, you may want to ask that payment be made.

Severance

In the event of termination, you need to understand any severance pay provisions. These are not common and most contracts provide only for payment of base salary through the date of termination.

More important in the event of early termination is how trailing incentive compensation is handled. For example, if incentive compensation is calculated and paid quarterly, what happens if the contract is terminated two months into the quarter? Is the incentive calculation prorated or are you simply out of luck?

Finally, consider how malpractice tail coverage will be handled in case of termination.

Governance, management and day-to-day operational roles

Many physicians seek hospital employment so they can avoid being involved in day-to-day management, group meetings, and other governance activities. Some physicians, on the other hand, actually welcome involvement in these roles. Either way, you want to be sure you understand what is required with respect to management and governance participation as part of the employment agreement and any potential impact these activities could have on your productivity and off-hours.

Some hospitals set aside funds in their incentive compensation that are paid to physicians who participate in governance, committee roles, and other management functions.

PUBLICITY

Many hospitals do not publicly announce or brand physicians as being part of the hospital. The approach to this issue varies greatly based on specific market competitive factors and even local custom. You may want to understand the hospital's strategy here, but don't expect too much control over how it chooses to promote or brand the practice.

Takeaway Points for Chapter 5

1. Hospital acquisition of a physician practice generally consists of two components: an asset purchase agreement and an employment agreement. The employment agreement is generally much more important than the asset purchase agreement.
2. Base salary and incentive compensation post-sale are by far the most important aspects of selling your practice.
3. The employment agreement will typically provide for a base salary, likely based on your historical earnings. Sometimes the base salary is guaranteed for a period of time, usually no longer than one or two years, but will still include productivity standards.
4. Most employment contracts require some level of productivity be maintained to earn the base salary.
5. Incentive compensation is one of the most important components of your post-sale employment. It can also be one of the most complex.

6. Profit-based incentives have become the most common type of incentive plan because they, by their very nature, protect hospitals from losing money on physician practices.

7. Hospitals will typically offer a high percentage of profits to the physicians: 50% is typical but I've see the incentive percents go as high as 90%.

8. The weakness of a productivity-based incentive from the hospital perspective is that it provides no incentive for the physicians to control costs.

9. Enterprise incentive plans can be very lucrative, but they effectively put incentive compensation out of the direct control of individual physicians and rely instead on broader goals and group-wide objectives.

10. Most employment agreements provide for termination with cause. Care needs to be taken in how the cause is defined and who makes the determination.

11. Some hospitals, seeking to avoid these conflicts, are offering termination without cause provisions. These provisions generally provide that either party, on giving required notice (usually 90 to 180 days) can terminate the relationship for any reason.

12. Termination-without-cause provisions often have the opposite effect: Rather than resulting in hasty terminations, they provide the parties a pathway to work together in resolving issues and strengthening the relationship.

13. Most employment agreements are going to include some kind of non-compete provision. While this may seem offensive, absent a non-compete provision your practice has no value to the hospital.

14. Time, distance, and geographic location parameters included in most restrictive covenants are often negotiable and need to be considered in the context of your practice's service area, demographics, and competitive environment. These issues need to be considered carefully because you may be putting your future ability to practice in the area at risk if it doesn't work out.

15. Many physicians seek hospital employment so they can avoid being involved in day-to-day management. Make sure you understand what is required with respect to management and governance and any potential impact these activities could have on your productivity and off-hours.

CHAPTER 6

Negotiations

During a negotiation, it would be wise not to take anything personally.
If you leave personalities out of it, you will be able to see opportunities
more objectively.   BRIAN KOSLOW

I f you've properly prepared your practice for sale as described in Chapter 2, you
should have maximized your value and have a practice the hospital should be
very interested in acquiring.

If you've done your homework in Chapter 3, you should have chosen a hospital that
is financially stable and has a commitment to successful practice management.

You should also have a good idea of what your practice is worth from Chapter 4
and a good understanding of the deal structure and compensation pitfalls from
Chapter 5.

So enter into formal negotiations with a high level of confidence. Now you're ready
to make your case that the robustness of your business makes you an attractive candidate to fit into the hospital's strategy.

THE ROLE OF OUTSIDE ADVISORS

Many physicians have told me over the years: "Physicians aren't very good at business." My retort is that people in business make even worse physicians. I have worked
with many physicians who are actually very astute at business. In my experience, the
danger is in physicians who *think* they are astute when they aren't.

I'll leave it to you decide where you fit in this equation, but remember the old
adage in the legal profession that an attorney who represents himself has a fool for
a client. This adage has a lesson for physicians as well.

You will need a good healthcare attorney to review the agreements and make sure
your interests are protected. Most practices have an attorney they consult on general business matters, but healthcare has its own unique legal issues. I've been in
meetings with very experienced attorneys whose dismal lack of healthcare experience
borders on malpractice when advising their clients on a practice sale. They treat the
sale as any other business transaction, often to the detriment of their client.

Don't get your attorney involved too early. Usually you don't need an attorney before you have a formal offer and draft asset purchase and employment agreements for review. Many of the business points of the deal are likely not up for negotiation. Hospitals with experience in buying physician practices and employing physicians generally have a model they follow and are unlikely to vary from it in any major way.

You need to focus your efforts on things that are important to you in the longer term, such as base salary, productivity standards, incentive compensation, and input into management. To objectively evaluate these items, you probably will need a practice consultant.

You may already have a trusted practice consultant you can rely on to help you through the process. Many CPA firms provide excellent consulting services to their clients, but some don't. Most CPAs view themselves as consultants but, like attorneys, finding one with the specialized expertise you really need isn't always that easy. Here, too, experience is the key component.

There are many excellent independent practice consulting firms as well. If you don't know where to start, ask some of your physician colleagues or check with your local medical society. The hospital may also be able to make a referral to an experienced firm.

In my experience, one thing above all that exposes an inexperienced advisor—be it an attorney or consultant—is an almost singular focus on price, i.e., the value of your practice. Inexperienced advisors often do not understand the nuances and perspective of the parties and often seek to show their worth by trying to get a higher price for your practice. While price is important, there are often other, more important, considerations.

Avoid practice brokers: Most are simply seeking to gain their commission, which is generally a percentage of the sales price. Therefore, they focus solely on price with little or no expertise or understanding of the all-important post-sale issues.

The cost of hiring legal and consulting professionals often comes into play here as well. You get what you pay for and all advisors aren't created equal. Back in the '90s, it was fairly common for the acquiring hospital to reimburse the physician at closing for legal and consulting fees. That is uncommon this time around. Don't forget, you are talking about your livelihood here, and it is in your best interest to spend a few thousand dollars to protect yourself and fully understand the implications of what is being proposed.

INITIAL HOSPITAL MEETING

After the valuation of your practice has been completed, there will be a meeting where the hospital is expected to make its initial offer. It is usually best to view this meeting as a preliminary sales meeting where the hospital is making its sales presentation, so your attorney or consultant would generally not attend. The tone of this meeting will change if advisors are present asking detailed questions. When in doubt, ask the hospital what the agenda for the meeting is and then make your decision.

Make sure this meeting is scheduled at a time when you will not be distracted by the need to get back to work and that your schedule is flexible in case the meeting runs over. Ask for an agenda for the meeting in advance, and don't be afraid to set out what you expect to be covered (checklists in this chapter and in Chapter 7 may help you).

Sometimes this meeting turns out to be disappointing in its lack of details and substance. There can be many reasons for this. Sometimes the hospital hasn't had adequate time to prepare. Sometimes it is simply trying to gauge your interest or gather additional information about your motivations and plans. For example, a question often asked in the hospital administrative suite is what is motivating a physician to sell. Is he or she interested in retiring early or in slowing down? Is the reason given for wanting to sell the "real" reason, or is there some other hidden agenda that needs to be ferreted out?

Anticipate these questions and be clear at the outset about your needs and desires. Always act in good faith and be honest about your intentions. There are no secrets in medical communities.

Before you go into this meeting, you should take some time with your practice consultant to sketch out, at least on a preliminary basis, the major components of an acceptable deal. Emotions have no place here. If you've completed the valuation worksheet in Chapter 4, you should have a ballpark idea of the value of your practice, what level of salary and bonus structure would be acceptable, and what other terms and conditions are important to you. This initial meeting isn't the time to bring these up, because you will just be learning the hospital's assumptions, etc.

In negotiation meetings, physicians often wear their emotions on their sleeve and talk too much. The hospital representatives may ask what would be an acceptable price for your practice or an acceptable compensation. Play your cards close to the vest. There's no upside in telling the hospital how much you think your practice is worth or what salary you think it should offer at this point.

During this initial meeting, maintain a calm demeanor and listen. A hospital acquiring your practice is, at its core, about creating value through the combination of efforts. Negotiation, therefore, will ultimately center on who claims that value.

Physicians often focus too much on the value of their practice. Generally your compensation is much more important. When hospitals bought practices in the '90s, they offered physicians large, long-term, guaranteed base salaries. Then they watched physician productivity plummet by an average of 20–25%. Hospitals learned their lesson, so don't expect the security of a long-term guaranteed contract. Expect a base salary typically based on prior-year earnings and guaranteed, if at all, only for a relatively short period such as one or two years. Expect that meeting productivity standards will be a part of the guarantee.

The value of your practice is, in general, not up for a lot of negotiation. The hospital is limited to the value as determined by the independent valuation firm, so negotiation on the valuation usually is limited to areas where underlying assumptions were not correct. Many hospitals will decline to share the valuation report with you, but some will. It doesn't hurt to ask, as it can provide some insight to the valuation assumptions. Being able to challenge those assumptions may provide some ammunition for the negotiating that may happen later.

As discussed in Chapter 4, the assumptions made by the appraiser impact the value of your practice and the compensation being offered. Your goal during this initial meeting should be to gather as much information as possible and learn what these assumptions are. It may be possible to have the assumptions reevaluated if they do not fairly reflect the financial performance of the practice, but not at this initial meeting. Gather data, ask questions, and plan to come back later fully armed.

The questions you should ask at this first meeting will be dependent on the level of detail the hospital gets into. Here is a list of some potential questions you should be prepared to ask if the hospital discusses your practice's valuation and proposed compensation, and a brief discussion of each:

1. What is the projected revenue of the practice over the first few years after acquisition?

    The valuation firm will likely base this number on your historical revenue. If your recent historical revenue was lower or higher because of unusual circumstance, ask if those circumstances were considered. Common examples include changes in providers, such as the hiring or departure of an associate physician or mid-level provider; changes in work days for personal reasons, such as illness or injury; or the recent addition of a new ancillary service that may not be fully reflected in last year's income statement.

Billing and collection problems can also have an impact on these assumptions. While you may hesitate to admit your practice has had operational issues, it will ultimately be to your benefit to make sure the revenue reflects the true revenue-producing ability of your practice.

2. What is the projected revenue growth rate in the practice, and what is it based on?

The valuation firm will likely project future revenue growth based on either your practice's historical growth or the regional or national growth trends in your specialty. You should know your practice's historical revenue growth trend and any reasons why this growth was less than what you expect in the future. Demonstrating an understanding of your practice's finances can never hurt, and false assumptions can sometimes be changed if supported by concrete data.

3. What method was used to value my furniture and equipment?

The typical methods used were described in Chapter 4 and, in most cases, they don't make a lot of difference. At this stage you are gathering information. Refrain from judgments.

If the value of your furniture and equipment is significantly different than the estimate you gained from the worksheets in Chapter 4, ask if it would be possible to get an itemized list of furniture and equipment to review for completeness. While many hospitals won't share the complete valuation report, most will provide the furniture and equipment listing and related valuation.

Discussions at the initial meeting should also include issues such as what operational changes will take place post-sale. This discussion will supplement your earlier research in choosing a hospital. A desirable hospital partner will have clearer answers about post-sale operational issues, because they have experience in dealing with these issues in previous acquisitions and experience in practice management.

Don't be put off by nonspecific answers either. It is not unusual for hospitals to be examining many potential acquisitions simultaneously and the final answer as to how these will be integrated is often something driven by timing. What you are looking for is some substance and an indication that these items have been or are being given serious consideration.

Finally, consider whom you are meeting with. The hospital CEO may not be the most well versed member of hospital management to address some of these issues. Hospitals experienced in practice acquisitions and physician employment will have professional practice management personnel attending the meeting. These people are usually more capable of addressing these detail questions.

Timing is an important question you should be prepared to discuss at this initial meeting. There always seems to be a propensity, often driven by both sides, to "get the deal done." This is not always in your best interest. For example, if your bonus is dependent on cash collections, rushing the deal through without providing adequate time for transfer of provider numbers and payor credentialing will likely result in both disappointing first-year performance and diminished bonuses.

Overanxiousness on your part to get the deal done in an unrealistic time frame can also be construed as a sign your practice is faltering or, even worse, construed as a sign of negotiating weakness.

Take notes, but it is usually best to refrain from expressing strong opinions. At this stage, the hospital likely will not be presenting formal legal agreements. You should, however, expect the hospital to provide a nonbinding term sheet outlining the major terms of the proposed offer. If one isn't provided, ask that one be provided within a short period of time after the meeting.

Ask that the term sheet be specific to your practice and include a detailed description of base salary, productivity standards, and incentive compensation. Ask for an example of how incentive compensation is calculated to aid you and your advisors in understanding what is being proposed.

Try to leave the first meeting with a second meeting scheduled and firm deadlines for the hospital to get back to you with answers to your questions and any additional items it promises to provide as a result of the meeting. Make sure that it provides the information promised enough in advance to allow you to review and react to its written responses.

NEGOTIATING STRATEGY

After the initial meeting you should have the hospital's initial offer. Now it is time for you to step back for some deliberate consideration and strategizing.

Compare the offer to your initial expectations. If it is significantly different, you may want to work with your practice consultant to break down the differences. Use the Chapter 4 valuation worksheet to raise additional questions.

The answers to the questions you asked in the initial meeting and the comparison to your initial expectations should provide some insight as to how the hospital and its valuation firm arrived at their initial offer. While your practice's value may not be negotiable, understanding and challenging the underlying assumptions can result in a revised offer that may more closely reflect your expectations.

Here is a list of major issues that may need further review and clarification:

Asset value

Compare the asset value offered to your expectation. Review the equipment list and values for completeness. While the valuation method generally isn't negotiable, errors and omissions in the asset list should be updated. In addition, some major items can have values well in excess of the typical valuation methods used (as described in Chapter 4). Examples include ophthalmology and imaging equipment such as ultrasound machines, x-ray equipment, CT scanners, etc.

Practice value

If the practice has no business enterprise value, make sure you understand the assumptions used in the financial projections. The worksheet in Chapter 4 should be used here to highlight issues for discussion. As noted above, most hospitals will not share the valuation report, but they will answer your questions on issues such as projected revenue growth, overhead growth, and post-sale provider compensation.

Base salary

Make sure you understand how the base salary offer was determined and what, if any, productivity standards are required to earn that salary. Base salary and the period it is guaranteed, if any, is often negotiable.

Incentive compensation

Be sure you understand the incentive compensation methodology and have been provided both a written description and a sample calculation. Pay close attention to where the numbers come from and how they relate to your current performance.

Follow-up hospital meetings

There may be other minor issues that need clarification as well. At this point, negotiations generally go back and forth. The hospital may engage its advisors in these discussions. Depending on the nature and importance of the issues, it may be appropriate at this point for your advisors to attend these meetings as well.

Maintain a list or log of negotiating points and keep track of the status of each one. An example of this log is included at the end of this chapter along with a sample form.

You may wish to include questions from Chapter 7 in your discussions with the hospital (see Chapter 7 checklist).

REACHING A DECISION POINT

At some point the time will come when you realize what is on the table is about the best you're going to do. You should be able to recognize, by how the hospital handled the negotiations, how well-versed and experienced they are in practice acquisitions. Even though you may not have gotten everything you wanted, the insight you gain from the negotiations and their explanations of various issues should tell you the rest of what you need to know to make your final decision.

Maybe that decision is clear. If it isn't, take some time now to read through Chapter 8: Options Other Than Selling. These options (and your willingness to invest the time, effort, and money in pursuing them) may aid you in coming to a final decision.

HOSPITAL PERSPECTIVE

Most hospitals find inexperienced attorneys and consultants exasperating to deal with. Sometimes advisors take on what I like to call the role of "the unwinder." An unwinder is simply someone who could be acting to protect a vested interest—in this case a long-standing client. Objective advisors will do their best to understand a physician's motivations to sell and help the physician understand if the post-sale results will meet those needs.

I have seen attorneys create unwarranted adversarial situations, and I've seen hospitals simply walk away. At its core, the sale of a practice is a common and straightforward business transaction. There are many physicians clamoring to sell and, as noted above, it is a buyer's market in many areas. At some point the hospital may lump you in with your inappropriately troublesome attorney and decide purchasing your practice is simply not worth the trouble.

The best strategy is the deliberate approach I have advocated. Hospitals respect physicians who know their practice and are reasonable in their negotiations. Unreasonable demands and threats to redirect referrals if you don't get what you want are not negotiating strategies. They are soliciting an illegal inducement and will give hospitals another reason to walk away.

Takeaway Points for Chapter 6

1. You will need a healthcare attorney experienced in practice sales to review the agreements and make sure your interests are protected.

2. You also will need an experienced healthcare consultant.

3. Don't get your attorney involved too early. Usually you don't need an attorney until you have a formal offer and draft asset purchase and employment agreements for review.

4. It is in your best interest to spend a few thousand dollars to hire experienced advisors to protect yourself and help you fully understand the implications of what is being proposed.

5. After the valuation of your practice has been completed, there will be a meeting where the hospital is expected to make its initial offer. Before you go into this meeting you should take some time with your practice consultant to sketch out, at least on a preliminary basis, the major components of an acceptable deal.

6. Physicians often focus too much on the value of their practice. Generally your compensation is much more important.

7. The value of your practice is generally not up for a lot of negotiation. The hospital is limited to the value as determined by the independent valuation firm.

8. Many hospitals will decline to share the valuation report with you, but some will. It doesn't hurt to ask, as it can provide some insight to the valuation assumptions and may provide you some ammunition for negotiating later.

9. Your goal during the initial post-valuation meeting should be to gather as much information as possible and learn what the underlying assumptions are. It may be possible to have the assumptions reevaluated if they do not fairly reflect the financial performance of the practice. Gather data, ask questions, and plan to come back later fully armed.

10. Ask that the hospital provide a nonbinding term sheet outlining the major terms of the proposed offer. It should include a detailed description of base salary, productivity standards, and incentive compensation. Ask for an example of how incentive compensation is calculated to aid you and your advisors in understanding what is being proposed.

11. After you have the hospital's initial offer, step back for some deliberate consideration and strategizing. Compare the offer to your initial expectations. If it is significantly different, you may want to work with your practice consultant to break down the differences.

12. Maintain a list or log of negotiating points and keep track of the status of each one.

13. You should be able to recognize—by how the hospital handled the negotiations—how well-versed and experienced they are in practice acquisitions. The

insight you gain from the negotiations and its explanations of various issues should tell you the rest of what you need to know to make your final decision.

14. If the decision isn't clear, read through Chapter 8: Options Other Than Selling. These options and your willingness to invest the time, effort, and money in pursuing them, may aid you in coming to a final decision.

Example Negotiating Log

Issue	Equipment value
Description	Doesn't include new furniture purchased this year; hospital indicated they would update value on provision of documentation.
Action/Status	June 3: Provided hospital copies of invoices.
Expected Resolution	Hospital should agree to increase equipment value to reflect the $8,900 cost of these items.

Issue	Base salary
Description	Base salary offered is based on last year's income which was down as a result of billing issues that have been resolved this year.
Action/Status	Provided hospital charge and collection data for the past 18 months to show improvement.
Expected Resolution	Hospital should revise projections and base salary on updated numbers reflecting the current year's trend.

Issue	Incentive compensation
Description	Incentive is based on patient encounters. Need to understand how encounters target was established and how it relates to my practice's historical data.
Action/Status	Hospital is to provide written definition and worksheet showing its calculation of my encounters last year.
Expected Resolution	Encounter target needs to be based on the above calculation and contractual definition needs to match calculation.

Negotiating Log Form

Issue	
Description	
Action/Status	
Expected Resolution	

Issue	
Description	
Action/Status	
Expected Resolution	

Chapter 6 Checklist 1: The Initial Hospital Meeting

After the valuation of your practice has been completed, there will be a meeting where the hospital is expected to make its initial offer. Although no checklist can be entirely comprehensive, this checklist covers the many of the steps you should take.

Prior to the Initial Meeting

Take some time with your practice consultant to sketch out, at least on a preliminary basis, the major components of an acceptable deal:

1. A ballpark idea of the value of your practice (see Chapter 4 worksheet)
2. What level of salary and bonus structure would be acceptable
3. Other terms and conditions that are important to you

During the Initial Meeting

Your goal during the initial post-valuation meeting should be to gather as much information as possible.

1. Learn the underlying assumptions the hospital used for their calculations. It may be possible to have the assumptions reevaluated if they do not fairly reflect the financial performance of the practice.
2. Gather data, ask questions, and plan to come back later fully armed.
3. When the hospital discusses your practice valuation and proposed compensation (at this meeting or later), ask these questions if they are not already answered:
   - What is the projected revenue of the practice over the first few years after acquisition?
   - What is the projected revenue growth rate in the practice, and what is it based on?
   - What method was used to value my furniture and equipment?
   - What operational changes will happen post-sale? (Please see Chapter 7 checklists)
   - What is the general, expected timing for purchase? Does it allow adequate time for transfer of provider numbers and payor credentialing?
4. During the meeting or soon afterward, ask that the hospital provide the following:
   - A nonbinding term sheet outlining the major terms of the proposed offer. It should include a detailed description of base salary, productivity standards, and incentive compensation.

- An example of how incentive compensation is calculated, to aid you and your advisors in understanding what is being proposed.
- An appointment time for the next meeting.
- Agreed-on deadlines for further information the hospital will provide to you.

After the Initial Meeting

Once you have the hospital's initial offer, step back for some deliberate consideration and strategizing.

1. Compare the offer to your initial expectations (Chapter 4 worksheet). If it is significantly different, you may want to work with your practice consultant to break down the differences.
2. Maintain a list or log of negotiating points and keep track of the status of each one. (See Example Negotiating Log Forms.)
3. Review the insights you gained from the meeting and the hospital's explanations of various issues. These should help guide you as you make your final decision to proceed or not.

Operational and Post-Sale Issues

*All marriages are happy. It's the living together afterward that causes all
the trouble.*   RAYMOND HULL

A s difficult and time consuming as it can be to get the deal done, a myriad of
issues can arise after the sale as well. Problems these issues create can be
minimized if they are addressed during the sale process, so be sure to include
questions from this chapter in your discussions with the hospital.

The biggest issues post-sale usually take place during the transition from independent practice to hospital-owned. In every sale transaction there is a closing,
where everyone signs the agreements, funds change hands, and an effective date
is established. The effective date is often the day after closing. Everything from
the effective date forward such as billing, personnel, payroll, benefits, accounts
payable, and accounting are now legally the responsibility of your new employer,
the hospital.

All of these issues should be considered prior to the effective date and both parties should have an understanding of how they will be handled.

TIMING

As noted earlier, often there is a drive in a practice sale to "get the deal done." This
is not always in the best interest of either party. This urgency just as often is driven
by the physicians as it is the hospital. Once you've made the decision to sell and negotiated your best deal, it is understandable that you're ready to get on with it.

Hospitals often have the same anxiousness: They've made their decision, too, and
often want to move on. Their business strategy may come into play as well. For example, if their strategy is to renegotiate payor contracts around their broader physician
network, they want that network in place as soon as possible.

The hospital may defer to your preference on determining the effective date. What
is an appropriate time frame will vary depending on the circumstances. For example, if practice billing is going to be moved on to the hospital's system, more time

may be needed for hardware and software installation and staff training than if current systems will remain in place.

The best approach with timing is to establish a reasonable effective date and predicate that date on milestones being met. Checklist 1 at the end of this chapter lists typical critical path items that need to be considered in establishing an effective date. A flexible effective date conditioned on identifiable milestones will serve both parties better than an artificial date that has to be adhered to at all costs.

TRANSITION ISSUES

Transitions are difficult by their nature: There are mounds of details that need to be dealt with. Many of the problems can be minimized with good advance planning and attention to detail. Let's look at some of the major issues and how to minimize these issues.

Provider numbers and payor credentialing

Provider numbers and payor credentialing is often a complex issue. What needs to be done varies significantly depending on the organizational structure of the hospital's ownership, ever-changing regulations, and even varying interpretations of those regulations by fiscal intermediaries.

Hospital administration is generally not well-versed in the detail requirements, so experienced personnel are important. Regardless, it is hard to push bureaucracies; they move at their own pace. Medicare usually isn't as big a potential problem as the commercial payors. Medicare allows retroactive billing, so even if it takes several months to get the paperwork straightened out, the money will eventually come in. This isn't true with most commercial payors.

Sometimes it seems as if commercial payors deliberately drag out the process, because they typically don't allow retroactive billing. If your effective date is before everything is completed, the payors know you'll likely continue to see their patients— effectively for free. So there is little incentive for them to cooperate. Rushing the effective date without everything in place plays right into their hands.

If the parties are pushing for an effective date without allowing a minimum of 60 days to complete the provider number and credentialing work (and 90 or 120 days is often more realistic), the potential losses are huge.

This is also where the structure of your incentive compensation is important. If the hospital insists on forging ahead and billing and collection problems result, you want to make sure your bonus is not based on those collections or profitability because their problems then inevitably impact your income. Even if the resulting billing and collection issues are not your fault and don't directly impact you bonus, hospital management may find itself having to explain unexpected operating losses that may taint your practice's reputation.

Staff issues

Your staff will be going through a transition, too, and they will likely have a lot of questions and concerns about their salaries, benefits, and job security. Their job descriptions and reporting lines may change as well.

Small medical practices usually have ripe rumor mills. It is unlikely you'll get to this point without having to address the rumor that you're selling to the hospital.

In an independent physician practice, the staff knows who the ultimate authority is—the physician owners. Once the sale to the hospital is complete, this is often less clear.

While many hospitals have a general hands-off policy on most day-to-day operational issues, many physicians sell their practices to be out from under these responsibilities. That can be a double-edged sword. Conflicts arise, and staff can get caught in the middle between the hospital's practice manager, to whom they technically report, and the physician, who is used to being in charge.

Even if the hospital has a hands-off policy on day-to-day operational issues, that doesn't mean nothing changes. While this issue varies depending on the legal structure the hospital uses, it is likely your staff are now employees of the hospital or one of its affiliated companies and therefore subject to the hospital's personnel policies. Hospitals are subject to employment laws from which most small practices are exempt, such as the Family and Medical Leave Act (FMLA).

Hospital personnel policies are likely more stringent and formalized. For example, there is likely a formal process that has to be followed before a staff member can be terminated. Staff evaluations are probably more formalized and mandatory. Work rules such as break time and overtime requirements are also likely to be less flexible.

Most hospitals have salary scales based on job classifications. Progress through these salary scales is often based on years of service. Future staff raises may be subject to these pay scales and the hospital's budgets. Hospitals generally have higher salary scales and more generous employee benefits. These additional costs can impact your overhead and incentive compensation as well.

The process for hiring staff may also become more complex. While it will likely be a relief to have the hospital source and screen candidates, the hiring process can sometimes seem slow and cumbersome.

Your staff will likely be most concerned about changes in their benefits. While in most cases fringe benefits such as health insurance and retirement benefits improve under hospital employment, problems can arise for long-term employees who have years of service that provide them with additional vacation and sick days. Hospitals sometimes refuse to grandfather these benefits. Staff may not like these changes, resulting in increased turnover.

Prior to the effective date, the hospital should schedule a meeting with your staff to explain their employee manual and answer staff questions on benefits and other changes. Often a formal staff orientation is required by hospital personnel policies.

Financial reports

Almost all physician practices use the cash basis of accounting, while hospitals report their financial results on the accrual basis. In the simplest terms, here is the difference: To a physician, cash collections equal revenue. To a hospital, revenue is what they expect to collect from gross charges.

Accounting is simply dividing the financial results of a business into artificial periods such as months, quarters, and years. Over the life of any business, cash and accrual accounting will ultimately lead to the same financial results. Problems always arise when hospitals try to get physicians to understand accrual accounting.

Most hospitals have learned this lesson and generally prepare separate financial reports for their employed physicians on a cash basis, but you should ask just to make sure.

Vendor payments

After the effective date, all your practice bills—such as utilities, rent, telephone, and supply purchases—become the responsibility of the hospital. As a practical matter, it is virtually impossible to get all your vendor accounts transferred into the hospital's name on the effective date.

While this usually isn't a major issue, it does mean that somebody has to be on top of these details to make sure the bills get paid on a timely basis and ultimately the funds get accounted for properly.

Generally, the hospital will handle the payments after the effective date. In cases where invoices include both pre- and post-sale charges, a list of payments is generally maintained along with an allocation of what is the practice's responsibility and what is the hospital's responsibility. Generally the totals are reconciled after 60 to 90 days, and any amounts due-to/due-from are settled and paid.

HOSPITAL PERSPECTIVE

Problems with post-sale issues tend to arise with inexperienced hospitals. Hospitals that have experience have systems and procedures in place to address these issues.

Inexperienced hospitals often default to doing things through existing hospital systems and bureaucracy. If the hospital you have chosen to affiliate with lacks experience, it is incumbent on you and your advisors to carefully work through the issues discussed in this chapter in advance. Inflexibility and inexperience are a bad combination. These issues can be critical to getting the relationship off to a good start and failure to adequately deal with them may even reach the level of causing you to revisit your decision.

Takeaway Points for Chapter 7

1. A myriad of issues can arise after the sale, and these can be minimized if they are addressed during the sales process.
2. There often is a drive in a practice sale to "get the deal done." This is not always in the best interest of either party.
3. A flexible effective date conditioned on identifiable milestones will serve both parties better than an artificial date that has to be adhered to at all costs.
4. If the parties are pushing for an effective date without allowing a minimum of 60 days—and 90 or 120 days is often more realistic—to complete the provider number and credentialing work, the potential losses are huge.
5. Your staff will be going through a transition, too, and they will likely have a lot of questions and concerns about their salaries, benefits, and job security.
6. Your staff are now employees of the hospital or one of its affiliated companies and likely subject to the hospital's personnel policies.
7. Prior to the effective date, the hospital should schedule a meeting with your staff to explain their employee manual and answer staff questions on benefits and other changes.
8. Problems always arise when hospitals try to get physicians to understand accrual accounting. Most hospitals have learned this lesson and generally prepare separate financial reports for their employed physicians on a cash basis, but you should ask just to make sure.

9. Somebody has to be on top of the detail of vendor payments to make sure the bills get paid on a timely basis and make sure that ultimately the funds get accounted for properly.

10. These issues can be critical to getting the relationship off to a good start, and failure to adequately deal with them may even reach the level of causing you to revisit your decision.

Chapter 7 Checklist 1: Critical Path Items in Establishing an Effective Date

❑ Payor credentialing
- Medicare number transfers
- Medicaid
- Commercial payors

❑ Personnel
- Staff informational meetings

❑ Staff orientation and/or policy manual review
- Benefit enrollment
- Payroll

❑ Billing system
- Hardware, software, and data line installation
- Demographic data transfer
- Staff training
- Revisions to financial policies

❑ Accounts payable
- Approval process
- Payment policies and procedures
- Vendor account transfers
- Pre- and post-sale invoice reconciliation plan

❑ Malpractice
- Tail premium if changing carriers
- Changes in coverage
- Other

Chapter 7 Checklist 2: Operational/Staff Issues to Discuss with the Hospital

❏ How will vendor payments be handled and by whom during the transitional first months?

❏ Can the hospital's financial reports be generated on a cash basis for physicians?

❏ Does the hospital have a "hands-off" or an "involved" policy for day-to-day operational issues concerning your staff? Does that align with your preference?

❏ How will your staff be informed about their salaries, benefits, and job security? Will the hospital schedule a meeting with your staff to explain their employee manual and answer staff questions on benefits and other changes?

❏ How will staff job descriptions and reporting lines change?

❏ How will benefits such as health insurance and retirement benefits improve or change under hospital employment? Problems can arise for long-term employees who have years of service that provide them with additional vacation and sick days. Does the hospital grandfather these benefits?

❏ Since your staff will likely be subject to the hospital's personnel policies, how are those policies more stringent and formalized? What is the process that has to be followed before a staff member can be terminated? How are staff evaluations handled? What are the work rules for things such as break time and overtime?

❏ Hospitals generally have higher salary scales for staff and more generous employee benefits, so how will these additional costs impact your overhead and incentive compensation?

❏ What is the hospital's process for hiring staff?

CHAPTER 8

Options Other Than Selling

Selling your practice is a big decision that will likely impact you the rest of your professional career. You may have endured a lengthy process and protracted negotiations and still have some nagging doubts. Are these real or just last-minute jitters?

Go back and review Chapter 1 and the reasons you originally decided to explore selling. Are these reasons still valid? Will the proposed deal likely solve these problems and meet your needs?

Make a list of your concerns with the proposed sale. Are the reasons quantitative—that is, are they based on the financial terms of the deal such as salary and practice value? Or are the reasons qualitative—that is, based on concerns about your chosen hospital partner? Qualitative issues are usually much more important than quantitative ones when it comes to long-term satisfaction.

You may decide that remaining independent is the best course of action and, if you've followed the steps in Chapter 2: Preparing Your Practice for Sale, you should have a good objective assessment of your practice.

This chapter is about other options or what you want to do differently in the future.

LEASE YOUR PRACTICE

In some cases, the hospital fit seems right but the differences come down to terms and price. If you feel, after taking an honest assessment of your practice's strengths, that the hospital's offer simply isn't adequate, one option may be to lease your practice to the hospital.

Leasing your practice can have some distinct benefits. The biggest benefit is that it isn't as permanent, so it may be easier to test the waters. A lease will typically have a finite term, often two or three years, so both sides have a date to work toward. At that point it can be much easier to get out if things aren't working out.

Leases can be done with an option to purchase at a later date, although it would still be subject to an independent valuation at that time. After a year or two, you may find that working for the hospital is going just fine and price may be less important.

Not all hospitals will be willing to offer a practice lease. A practice lease generally substitutes a lease agreement for the asset purchase agreement. The lease typically would include the practice's tangible assets and often the intangible assets as well.

Don't expect a financial windfall on the lease payments. A lease is basically a payment for the right to use the underlying assets for a finite period of time, so the aggregate lease payments are going to be less than an outright sale because, after the lease term, you will still own the assets.

The essence of a typical practice lease is that the hospital leases the practice from you and then contracts with you to provide physician services to the practice's patients for the term of the lease.

This agreement, often referred to as a professional services agreement, will function much like an employment agreement. You agree to provide services to the practice's patients for an agreed-upon payment.

In a lease arrangement, the hospital will typically take over the management of the practice and employ the staff in the same manner as if you had sold your practice.

A weakness in leasing your practice is that you typically cannot be part of the hospital's collective negotiation of payor contracts because technically you are not an employee of the hospital.

JOIN A MANAGEMENT SERVICES ORGANIZATION (MSO)

An MSO simply means contracting with an affiliate of the hospital for the management of your practice by their practice management department.

Many hospitals are offering practice management services to physicians using the same infrastructure they created to support the hospital's employed physicians. These services are often available on a fee basis, and physicians can often choose from a menu of services they wish to purchase such as billing and collections, human resources (including employment of staff), and other practice management services.

A hospital can't legally provide these services for less than fair market value, but this arrangement can result in a higher level of practice management expertise, often for the same or slightly higher cost.

The big weakness of an MSO is that it cannot collectively negotiate payor contracts for independent groups. An MSO can take away a majority of the day-to-day management burden and afford you the opportunity to try out the hospital's ability to manage your practice without taking the full step of selling.

The main difference between a practice lease and an MSO is in the area of compensation:

- In a lease the physician compensation is based on a predetermined payment (sometimes with an incentive) coupled with a payment for the lease of the practice assets.
- In an MSO arrangement the physician turns over management to the hospital but physician compensation is what is left after payment of the management fee.

TAKE YOUR PRACTICE TO THE NEXT LEVEL

You may have been happy and successful before the hospital came to call. If that's the case and the hospital's offer simply didn't meet your needs, staying independent isn't a daunting proposition.

If you approached the hospital or welcomed their advances because you were frustrated for some or all of the reasons mentioned in Chapter 1, then having the deal fall apart may leave you with a level of dread. If that's the case, go back and reread Chapter 2 on preparing your practice for sale. Take the information and insight you've gained by going through the sales process to chart a different course. (See Checklist at the end of this chapter).

For better or for worse, your practice is a small business. A medical license and hanging out your shingle isn't enough anymore. What did you learn about your practice's finances in Chapter 2 that you can improve? Why was your valuation less than you had expected in Chapter 4? What can you do to change those things? What is your strategic plan? What can you do to improve things and either make your practice a better candidate for sale in the future or make it thrive without the need to sell?

Based on 20-plus years working with physician practices, I have found that physician practices stagnate for the following reasons:

1. Aging providers who get comfortable with below-average income levels.
2. An entrenched practice manager (sometimes a spouse) whose skills haven't evolved with the needs of the modern-day practice.
3. Unwillingness to invest in experienced management and billing personnel.
4. An aging patient base, changing demographics in the practice's service area, and a deteriorating payor mix.
5. Fear of taking risks in practice expansion through additional physicians, mid-level providers, or ancillary services.

6. Bad experiences with former physician partners, associate physicians, or mid-level providers.
7. Lack of a business plan or strategy to address such things as service niches, ancillary services, mergers, and satellite offices.
8. Poor payor contract rates and lack of data, expertise, and willingness to negotiate better rates, coupled with an unwillingness to terminate marginal contracts.

In a group practice, I would add the following reasons:

1. Behavioral issues or personality clashes with one or more of the physicians.
2. A compensation plan that does not properly incentivize behavior.

If you find one or more of these things prevalent in your practice, the decision is clear: You can make some hard decisions or continue down your current path.

The biggest barrier to change is always the effort required to break habits and take risks. These may include incurring debt to invest in ancillary services or technology, recruiting new physician associates or mid-level providers, hiring a highly qualified (and highly paid) professional manager, or becoming more creative and proactive about promoting your practice.

If you go this route, consider engaging an outside consultant to work with your group on the following actions:

- Develop a comprehensive strategic plan
- Take the emotion out of these decisions, and keep you pointed in the right direction
- Follow through to make the changes needed to improve operations
- Monitor progress and keep you focused on results

MERGE WITH AN EXISTING LARGER GROUP

Many solo and small groups automatically shun the idea of joining an existing large group practice. This is often based on a bad experience earlier in their career.

Group practice today is much different that it was 10 or 20 years ago. Many long-standing "legacy" groups—groups that were established decades ago—are no longer in business. They had become victims of the practice management companies that failed in the '90s (Chapter 3) or had imploded under the weight of their own bureaucracy and management overhead. Those that still exist have been through major restructuring in order to survive.

Many areas of the country have larger group practices that have been created in the past 10 years. These groups are often progressive and successful, with income levels well-above national standards. They tend to operate on a model that allows a large degree of physician autonomy, avoids bloated management overhead, and employs aggressive ancillary and payor contracting strategies.

If you've been through the sales process with the hospital, you have already gained valuable knowledge about your business. Don't be scared off by past reputations or ancient history with a larger group—initiate discussions and go through the process to see if you find a better fit.

The process of merging your practice with an existing group is, in many ways, quite different than selling to a hospital, but there are similarities as well.

You will be asked to provide financial data on your practice, and you should expect them to provide the same data to you.

Just as income was a key component in selling your practice to a hospital, their income is the key component in deciding whether to join their group. Compare their incomes to yours and to the MGMA benchmarks you reviewed in Chapter 2.

Obviously, you are looking for their incomes to be materially higher than yours because, ultimately, their incomes represent your potential income post-merger.

Have your CPA or practice consultant review the financial information they provide if it seems too overwhelming to do yourself. If their incomes are higher, you will want to gain a basic understanding of why. Do they work more hours? See more patients? Offer more ancillary services?

Other questions you will want to examine include the following:

1. How does their overhead compare to yours in terms of dollars and percentage?
2. What will happen to your overhead when you join them?
3. Will your costs actually go up because they have higher staff salaries and benefit costs?
4. Will your office be consolidated into one of their locations?

The biggest potential prize in joining a large group is often in the payor contracts. It is unlikely the group will share specific information with you on their payor contracts prior to completion of the merger, because doing so may constitute illegal price fixing. Ask questions about their contracting expertise and abilities. The success of their contracts should be evident by looking at their income levels.

Existing groups virtually never purchase goodwill. Other physicians don't want to invest in your goodwill any more than you would want to invest in theirs. It is likely they will have a streamlined valuation process and simply offer to purchase your assets. If you went through the process with the hospital, you will have another reference point to determine the reasonableness of their offer.

Larger groups also generally have a predefined merger model that is probably not negotiable. Previous mergers were likely done under this same model and varying the model is usually not an option because the precedent has already been set.

You will generally be asked to sign an asset purchase agreement, employment agreement, and buy-sell (shareholders) agreement.

The employment agreement is similar in many ways to the hospital employment agreement discussed in Chapter 5. The most significant difference will be in the compensation sections.

Just as in selling to a hospital, the most important aspect is your compensation and bonus structure post-merger. Physician groups generally do not have guaranteed salaries and incentive compensation or bonus plans. Existing group practices have a predetermined method of compensating physician owners, often referred to as a compensation (or income distribution) plan.

The distinction is important but probably not surprising: There are no shareholder guarantees in a group practice anymore than there are in a solo practice or small group. Shareholder income is determined by the financial performance of the group.

The complexity of a group's compensation plan often increases with the size of the group. Multi-specialty group compensation plans tend to be complex. The group should provide you with a pro forma financial projection of how your practice would fit into the group's existing compensation plan and give you a fairly accurate estimate of what your income would be post-merger.

You should generally expect to come in as an equal owner in the group. Some larger groups, especially those with significant earnings streams coming from ancillary services, may not be willing to offer a newly merged physician a full share of those ancillary profits initially. This may be reasonable, depending on your specialty and the types of ancillaries involved.

Employment agreements with larger group practices generally contain a restrictive covenant. While it may seem counterintuitive, you want the group to have one and you should shy away from any group that doesn't.

A physician group is not really a group without some glue holding the physicians together. If people can leave at any time whenever a decision doesn't go their way, the group isn't sustainable. I have seen group practices collapse in short order absent a restrictive covenant.

The buy-sell (or shareholders) agreement is an agreement between all of the partners and provides how physicians join (buy) and leave (sell) their ownership in the practice. Generally the stock buyout will be a share of the value of the assets of the group.

Be wary of buy-sell agreements that provide for excessive buyout payments, deferred compensation, and other provisions for payments to physicians no longer practicing. While a huge golden parachute may sound attractive, the money has to come out of the work of those physicians still in practice.

Large buyout obligations are another reason group practices collapse because, at some point, it is easier to liquidate the group than continue to satisfy huge trailing obligations to physicians who have retired or otherwise left the group.

There are some business models for group practices out there that have a high probability of problems. Shy away from a group where everyone is not an equal shareholder with an equal vote in the affairs of the group. Group practices owned or controlled by one physician or even a small group of "insider" physicians are generally not sustainable.

Also stay away from groups with physician incomes lower than yours. Low incomes in large groups are often caused by bloated overhead, entrenched management, unproductive physicians, substandard billing and collections, and marginal payor contracts.

Out of necessity, large groups have a governance structure that usually consists of a Board of Directors who are elected by the shareholders to run the group. The Board generally is required to consult the shareholders before making major decisions such as borrowing money in excess of a certain dollar amount, major capital expenditures, hiring additional physicians, merging with other practices, terminating physicians, changing the compensation plan, and selling the group. These major decisions are often subject to supermajority votes of the shareholders.

Shareholder meetings generally must be held at least once a year, at which time the Board of Directors are elected. Quarterly meetings are common. Many physicians feel disenfranchised in larger groups because participation in governance is limited to Board members. Other physicians feel a relief in not having to be involved in the day-to-day decision-making.

Depending on the size of the group, the Board may also have standing committees that meet separately and report to the Board on issues such as finance, managed-care contracting, and compensation. Committee membership is often filled by non-board members, so if participating in the governance of the group is important to you, you will want to ask these types of questions.

MERGE WITH LIKE-MINDED COLLEAGUES

Becoming larger is one of the classic business strategies used to survive in a changing marketplace. A merger is like a marriage—smaller practices pool their resources for a more effective operation—and all successful marriages require compromises.

Many physicians show a surprising reluctance toward joining a larger group or merging their practices. There are many reasons for this including previous failed attempts, startup costs, risks, lack of guarantees, etc. In spite of these barriers, mergers are a viable alternative to selling to a hospital.

Mergers too often fail because they are approached the wrong way. Hiring a lawyer is the first thing most groups do when they decide to explore a merger. Lawyers don't "explore," they document.

The first step in merging with like-minded groups is exactly that—find like-minded groups. Single-specialty mergers are easier because physicians in the same specialty likely face the same challenges in their practices. For example, a couple of years ago I helped 30 pediatricians in eight groups explore a merger. It was fun to watch the camaraderie they established because they all faced the same problems unique to pediatrics.

Another thing I find in working with physicians on mergers is that their relationship with physicians in their specialty is often on a superficial professional level. Merging means going into business with one another, and the merger process is important because it allows physicians to get to know one another outside of a clinical setting.

One question that always comes up when creating a new group through merger is the question of size. How big should we be? How big do we need to be to impact payor contracting, or add new services, or hire a professional manager?

The answer is: It depends. I have formed several physician groups through mergers of more than 50 physicians. Some of those groups were extremely successful. Others were only marginal successes, because they failed to coalesce as a group and execute their business strategy.

The success of a merger is determined after the merger. It is driven by how well the new group executes its strategic plan. I have seen primary care groups as small as five impact payor rates and add profitable new services such as CT scanners to their offices. I have seen groups five times that size have little or no success with the same endeavors.

After you have identified like-minded colleagues to explore a merger, the next step is to find an experienced merger consultant. This is not as easy as it sounds.

Virtually every consultant and CPA firm working with physician practices will tell you they have experience in mergers. Take these claims with a grain of salt. Having once had one client who merged with another practice doesn't qualify as real experience in practice mergers.

Ask for references of groups of similar size and take the time to talk to the physicians about their merger experience. An experienced merger consultant will be glad to provide you a list of questions and discussion points.

Successful mergers have a good foundation. Your merger consultant should take you though discussions of your purpose, vision, motivations, and fears. They should complete a detailed financial assessment of each practice. You should also expect to spend a lot of time talking (without lawyers) about how you want to govern yourselves and manage your business.

Financial projections should be prepared combining all of the practices into one entity and overlaying changes that will be made as a result of the merger.

Avoid merger consultants who tout economies of scale as one of the big benefits of a merger. This, more than anything, shows a lack of experience. In most mergers, costs go up, at least initially and often permanently. This is because typically you are hiring a higher level of management and creating the management infrastructure necessary to manage a larger organization. Staffing cuts and other cost-cutting measures often do not materialize.

I have been involved in dozens of mergers involving hundreds of practices, and I have rarely seen overhead go down. Yet in spite of this increased overhead, I have seen revenue and physician incomes go up, often substantially, in a vast majority of mergers.

If overhead is projected to go down, make sure you have specifics. Which offices will be closed, which staff (by name) will be cut, and what other specific costs will be eliminated? It is easy to talk about cutting overhead in generalities, but it becomes much more difficult when you are forced to examine it at a detail level.

One area where practices can gain some economies in a merger is in the area of capital purchases. A good example is in information technology. Major economies can be gained in sharing the cost of practice management, billing, and EMR systems.

Another example is in shared ancillary service development such as the CT services mentioned above. The risk of buying a refurbished CT scanner, for say $100,000, may sound daunting to a solo or small group but sharing the cost (and risk) among 10 physicians is much more palatable.

Once you have examined the finances, you should have a firm idea of the potential financial downside. The decision usually comes down to how confident you are that this downside can be made up with additional revenue.

You are ready to hire an experienced merger attorney once you can answer the following questions:

1. What are the purpose, vision, and mission of the group?
2. How will the group govern itself, make decisions, resolve conflicts, and manage day-to-day operations?
3. What is the projected overhead for the first year post-merger?
4. How will the group divide income, and what is the projected post-merger income for each physician in the group?
5. What are three or four specific things the group plans to do in the first 12 months to increase revenue and by how much?

An experienced merger attorney will guide you through translating all the decisions you have made into formal legal language.

While the legal documents are being drafted, your merger consultant will take you and your staff through the operational implementation of the merger. This involves working through the myriad of detailed operational decisions that have to be made prior to the merger effective date.

You should generally allow six months or so for this operational implementation process. The caveats mentioned in Chapter 7 apply—don't get caught up in an artificial timetable to "get the deal done." The list of issues can be broadly categorized as follows:

- Provider numbers and payor credentialing
- Staff issues including employee benefits, personnel policies, etc.
- Accounting and finance

While the task of merging can be overwhelming at times, it has many potential rewards: a practice with your chosen like-minded colleagues that allows you to retain you autonomy and operate in a business model you designed specifically to meet you needs.

Takeaway Points for Chapter 8

1. You may have endured a lengthy process and protracted negotiations and still have some nagging doubts. Review the reasons you originally decided to explore selling. Will the proposed deal likely solve these problems and meet your needs?

2. Make a list of your concerns with the proposed sale. Are the reasons quantitative or qualitative? Qualitative issues are usually much more important than quantitative ones when it comes to long-term satisfaction.

3. If the fit seems right but the hospital's offer simply isn't adequate, one option may be to lease your practice to the hospital. A lease isn't as permanent, so it may be easier to test the waters.

4. If you decide that remaining independent is the best course of action, you should have gained a good objective assessment of your practice from Chapter 2.

5. An MSO can take away a majority of the day-to-day management burden and afford you the opportunity to try out the hospital's ability to manage your practice without taking the full step of selling.

6. You can make some hard decisions or continue down your current path. The biggest barrier to change is always the effort required to break habits and take risks.

7. If you decide to stay independent, you may need to incur debt to invest in your practice's growth. Consider engaging an outside consultant to work with your group to develop a comprehensive strategic plan, take the emotion out of these decisions, and keep you pointed in the right direction.

8. Consider merging with an existing larger group. Don't be scared off by past reputations or ancient history. Initiate discussions and go through their process—you might find a better fit.

9. You are looking for their incomes to be materially higher than yours because, ultimately, their incomes represent your potential income post-merger.

10. The biggest potential prize in joining a large group is often in the payor contracts. The success of their contracts should be evident by looking at their income levels.

11. Merging with like-minded colleagues is a viable alternative to selling to a hospital. While the task of merging can be overwhelming at times, it has many potential rewards: a practice with your chosen like-minded colleagues that allows you to retain you autonomy and operate in a business model you designed specifically to meet you needs.

Chapter 8 Checklist 1: Checklist for Taking Your Practice to the Next Level

Take the information and insight you've gained by going through the hospital's sales process to chart a different course. Here are a series of questions to help you get an overview of where you stand and where you may want to go:

1. What did you learn about your practice's finances in Chapter 2 that you can improve?
2. Why was your valuation less than you had expected in Chapter 4? What can you do to change those things?
3. What should be in your strategic plan to either make your practice a better candidate for sale in the future or make it thrive without the need to sell? Options could include the following actions:
   - Incurring debt to invest in ancillary services or technology
   - Recruiting new physician associates or mid-level providers
   - Hiring a highly qualified (and highly paid) professional manager
   - Becoming more creative and proactive about promoting your practice
4. Consider whether your practice has stagnated for any of following reasons and make notes. What action would need to be taken to correct problems?
   - Aging providers who get comfortable with below-average income levels
   - An entrenched practice manager (sometimes a spouse) whose skills haven't evolved with the needs of the modern-day practice
   - Unwillingness to invest in experienced management and billing personnel
   - An aging patient base and/or deteriorating payor mix
   - Fear of taking risks in practice expansion through additional physicians, mid-level providers, or ancillary services
   - Bad experiences with former physician partners, associate physicians, or mid-level providers
   - Lack of a business plan or strategy to address such things as service niches, ancillary services, mergers, and satellite offices.
   - Poor payor contract rates and lack of data, expertise, and willingness to negotiate better rates, coupled with an unwillingness to terminate marginal contracts
   - Behavioral issues or personality clashes in a group practice with one or more physicians
   - A group practice compensation plan that does not properly incentivize behavior

Chapter 8 Checklist 2: Merge with an Existing Larger Group

1. You will be asked to provide financial data on your practice, and you should expect them to provide the same data to you.

2. The larger group's income is the key component in deciding whether to join their group. Compare their incomes to yours and to the MGMA benchmarks you reviewed in Chapter 2. Their incomes represent your potential income post-merger.

3. Have your CPA or practice consultant review the financial information provided if it seems too overwhelming to do yourself. If their incomes are higher, you will want to gain a basic understanding of why:
   - Do they work more hours?
   - Do they see more patients?
   - Do they offer more ancillary services?

   Other questions you will want to examine include the following:
   - How does their overhead compare to yours in terms of dollars and percentage?
   - What will happen to your overhead when you join them?
   - Will your costs actually go up because they have higher staff salaries and benefit costs?
   - Will your office be consolidated into one of their locations?

4. Does the group have a streamlined valuation process to purchase your assets? Use your knowledge from the hospital as a reference point to determine the reasonableness of their offer.

5. What is the larger group's predefined merger model? Review their asset purchase agreement, employment agreement, and buy-sell (shareholders) agreement.

6. Physician groups generally do not have guaranteed salaries and incentive compensation or bonus plans, so review their compensation (or income distribution) plan. These can be complex, so the group should provide you with
   - A pro forma financial projection of how your practice would fit into the group's existing compensation plan
   - A fairly accurate estimate of what your income would be post-merger

7. Will you be an equal owner in the group? Some larger groups, especially those with significant earnings streams coming from ancillary services, may not be willing to offer a newly merged physician a full share of those ancillary profits

initially. This may be reasonable, depending on your specialty and the types of ancillaries involved.

8. Look for a restrictive covenant. A physician group is not really a group without some glue holding the physicians together. If people can leave at any time whenever a decision doesn't go their way, the group isn't sustainable.

9. The buy-sell (or shareholders) agreement is an agreement between all of the partners and provides how physicians join (buy) and leave (sell) their ownership in the practice. Generally the stock buyout will be a share of the value of the assets of the group. Be wary of buy-sell agreements that provide for excessive buyout payments, deferred compensation, and other provisions for payments to physicians no longer practicing.

10. The group probably will not be able to share specific information with you on their payor contracts prior to completion of the merger, because doing so may constitute illegal price fixing. Ask questions about their contracting expertise and abilities. The success of their contracts should be evident by looking at their income levels.

11. Shy away from a group where everyone is not an equal shareholder with an equal vote in the affairs of the group. Group practices owned or controlled by one physician or even a small group of "insider" physicians are generally not sustainable.

12. Also stay away from groups with physician incomes lower than yours.

13. Will you feel disenfranchised in larger groups because participation in governance is limited to Board members? Or will you feel a relief in not having to be involved in the day-to-day decision-making? Is membership on a committee an option or an obligation?

Chapter 8 Checklist 3: Merge with Like-Minded Colleagues

1. Hire a lawyer *after* you have explored options. Lawyers don't "explore," they document.

2. Find like-minded groups or physicians. Single-specialty mergers are easier because physicians in the same specialty likely face the same challenges in their practices.

3. Find an experienced merger consultant. Ask for references of groups of similar size and take the time to talk to the physicians about their merger experience. An experienced merger consultant will be glad to provide you a list of questions and discussion points.

4. With all parties, discuss your purpose, vision, motivations, and fears. Discuss how you want to govern yourselves and manage your business.

5. Each practice provides a detailed financial assessment. Financial projections should be prepared combining all of the practices into one entity and overlaying changes that will be made as a result of the merger.

6. Do not expect automatic "economies of scale." In most mergers, costs go up, at least initially and often permanently. You are typically hiring a higher level of management and creating the management infrastructure necessary to manage a larger organization.

7. If overhead is projected to go down, make sure you have specifics. Which offices will be closed, which staff (by name) will be cut, and what other specific costs will be eliminated? It is easy to talk about cutting overhead in generalities, but it becomes much more difficult when you are forced to examine it at a detail level.

8. One place to gain some economies in a merger is in the area of capital purchases, such as information technology. Another possibility is in shared ancillary service development.

9. You are ready to hire an experienced merger attorney once you can answer the following questions:
   - What are the purpose, vision, and mission of the group?
   - How will the group govern itself, make decisions, resolve conflicts, and manage day-to-day operations?
   - What is the projected overhead for the first year post-merger?
   - How will the group divide income, and what is the projected post-merger income for each physician in the group?

- What are three or four specific things the group plans to do in the first 12 months to increase revenue and by how much?

An experienced merger attorney will guide you through translating all the decisions you have made into formal legal language.

10. Operational implementation is the next step. This involves working through the myriad of detailed operational decisions that have to be made prior to the merger effective date. You should generally allow six months or so for this operational implementation process with details such as the following:
    - Provider numbers and payor credentialing
    - Staff issues including employee benefits, personnel policies, etc
    - Accounting and finance

Index